CONTENTS

FROM LENIN TO STALIN

VICTOR SERGE

translated from the French
by Ralph Manheim

Note on Translation: *From Lenin to Stalin* was translated by Ralph Manheim. *Life and Culture in 1918* was translated by Dan Eastman. *Lenin and Imperialism* was translated by "International Press Correspondence" (*Inprecorr*). *The End of Henry Yagoda* and *Stalin's Terror Continues with Envoy's Recall* were translated by *Socialist Appeal. The Conditions of Women* and *Managed Science, Literature, and Pedagogy* were translated by Max Shachtman.

First Edition, 1937
Second Edition, 1973
Fourth Printing, 1987

Published by the Anchor Foundation, Inc.

Distributed by Pathfinder Press
410 West Street, New York, New York 10014
Africa, Europe, and the Middle East:
    Pathfinder Press, 47 The Cut, London SE1 8LL, England
Asia, Australia, and the Pacific:
    Pathfinder Press, P.O. Box 37, Leichhardt,
    Sydney, NSW 2040, Australia
Canada:
    DEC Book Distribution, 229 College St., Toronto,
    Ontario M5T 1R4, Canada
New Zealand:
    Pilot Books, Box 8730, Auckland, New Zealand

A NOTE ABOUT THE AUTHOR

Victor Serge (Victor Lvovich Kibalchich) was born in Brussels on December 30, 1890, of parents who were Russian revolutionary emigres. His father had been an officer and later a physician, and was a sympathizer of the Narodnaya Volya (People's Will) Party. One of his relatives, a chemist belonging to this party, was hanged in 1881 after the assassination of Czar Alexander II.

Serge's childhood was spent in Belgium and England. One of his younger brothers died of want. At fifteen he was apprenticed to a photographer in Brussels. Later he became successively a photographer, a draftsman, an office worker, a linotype operator — after he had learned the trade in anarchist print shops — a journalist, and a translator. . . . At fifteen, he became a member of the socialist *Jeune Garde* in Ixelles; then a militant member of the *Groupe Revolutionnaire* in Brussels. He contributed to the *Temps Nouveaux, Libertaire*, and *Guerre Sociale*. He took part in demonstrations and trials. He spent some time in company villages in the north of France and took part in militant activity in Paris. Editor of *l'Anarchie* in 1910, during the period of illegality, he was arrested but refused to denounce the members of the underground group, of whom several killed themselves and others died on the guillotine. He was convicted under the infamous laws then in force and condemned to five years imprisonment. After being freed in 1917, he became a linotypist in Barcelona, a member of the CNT (Confederacion Nacional del Trabajo), a contributor to *Tierra y Libertad,* and took part in the first revolutionary attempt of July 1917. He then left for Russia, but was arrested in Paris and interned by the Clemenceau government in a concentration camp. He was exchanged in January 1919, as a Bolshevik hostage, for an officer in the French Military Mission, who was being held in Russia, and finally arrived in Petrograd.

5

He became a member of the Russian Communist Party and a colleague of Zinoviev on the Executive Committee of the Communist International during the civil war. He then became a gunner in a special battalion, a member of the military defense staff, and commissar of archives in the secret police under Krassin in 1919. He participated in the first congresses of the CI and became editor of the *Communist Internationl.* He spent considerable time in Germany (during the preparation of the 1923 uprising) and in Austria.

Serge returned to the Soviet Union in 1926 and publicly embraced the position of the Left Opposition. The smashing of the Opposition brought Serge's expulsion from the Communist Party, a brief period of imprisonment as a warning, and permanent blacklisting as far as employment was concerned. Already possessed of a literary reputation in France as a translator of Lenin and Trotsky and for his novels, pamphlets, and articles about revolutionary Russia, he now depended on his pen and the sale of his writings to French publishers and periodicals to support himself and his family. This was a very sparse and precarious livelihood, frustrating because of the Soviet censorship and postal authorities who delayed interminably or frequently "lost" his manuscripts even though they did not deal with contemporaneous political matters.

In 1933 he was again arrested and deported to Orenburg, a remote town on the Ural River. There he was soon joined by his young son Vlady. In France a campaign on Serge's behalf had been started in intellectual circles. It enlisted the support of a number of prominent literary figures, several of whom are reputed to have raised the question in audiences granted them by Stalin. Agitation about Serge became an embarrassment to Soviet diplomats and French Communist Party leaders, who with the change in line towards a popular front were assiduously wooing liberal and democratic support. In April 1936, Serge was allowed to leave the USSR for Belgium. He had got out by the skin of his teeth, the last person identified with opposition to Stalin to do so, for in July began the mass arrests, opening the great purges, and the first Moscow trial was staged in August.

In the initial period of his return to Western Europe, Serge collaborated with Leon Trotsky and his supporters, particularly in exposing the falseness of the Moscow Trials and making known the true situation in the Soviet Union. But he soon developed political differences with Trotsky, some of them on theoretical matters but most importantly on the policy of the POUM (Partido Obrero dé Unificacion Marxista — Workers Party of Marxist Unification) in the Spanish Revolution and Civil War. Serge ardently defended the POUM policy which Trotsky bitterly condemned as centrist. Thereafter Serge continued his political activity and writing, principally in the circles and press of the social democratic left. Forced to flee France after the Nazi victory, Serge and his family found asylum in Mexico, arriving there after Trotsky's assassination. Though he had plans to return to Europe, Serge died in Mexico on November 17, 1947.

* * *

Only part of Serge's writings have been translated into English. The historical and political works among these are *From Lenin to Stalin, Russia Twenty Years After* (title of British edition: *Destiny of a Revolution*), *Memoirs of a Revolutionary,* and *The Year One of the Russian Revolution.* His translated novels are *Men in Prison,* which is based on his five years in French jails; *Birth of Our Power,* drawing on his experiences in the Barcelona uprising of 1917, French internment camps, and Russia in the throes of civil war; *The Long Dusk,* picturing the fate of the refugees after the fall of France to the Nazi army; and *The Case of Comrade Tulayev,* based on Stalin's purge and the Moscow Trials.

His works available only in French, in addition to numerous pamphlets and magazine articles, include three novels: *Ville Conquise* [Conquered City], whose setting is Petrograd in 1919; *S'il Est Minuit dans le Siecle* [If It Is Midnight in the Century] describing the life of the deported and jailed Oppositionists in the USSR; *Les Annees sans Pardon* (The Years Without Reprieve), a novel in four sections which deals with prewar France, the Nazi siege of Leningrad, the fall of Hitler's Germany, and political refugees in Mexico.

Other works available only in French include *Litterature et Revolution, Portrait de Staline, Carnets* [Notebooks] covering the years 1936-38 and 1942-47, and *Vie et Mort de Trotsky* (Life and Death of Trotsky). Recently a volume of his poetry has been reissued under the title *Pour un brasier dans un desert* [For a Fire in a Wilderness]. One book *Hitler contra Stalin,* printed in Mexico City, exists only in Spanish.

Three other works are lost until the archives of the Soviet secret police are opened, since the manuscripts of these were confiscated from Serge before he left the Soviet Union in 1936. These are *L'An II de la Revolution Russe* [The Year II of the Russian Revolution], dealing with War Communism; *Les Hommes Perdus* [The Lost Men], a memoir of the pre-World War I anarchist movement; and *La Tourmente* [The Tempest], a novel about Russia in 1920.

From Lenin to Stalin

MARCH 1917

THE HEADLESS REVOLUTION

The entire first phase of the Russian Revolution seems to me today to have been dominated by the utter honesty of Lenin and his group. It was this that attracted all of us to him, regardless of our nationality and our viewpoint. In Spain early in 1917, I discussed the Russian Revolution with a group of militants who were even then talking of seizing Barcelona and setting up a new Commune (one day in July we posted its program on the walls). Salvador Segui, one of the founders of the CNT, whose portrait I have drawn as closely as I could in my novel, *Birth of Our Power* (he was assassinated two years after our conversation), questioned me on the subject of Bolshevism, which was fast becoming the world's greatest anxiety and its greatest hope. We were not Marxists, yet in the distorted echoes of Lenin's words that reached us, we could discern a remarkable integrity.

"Bolshevism," I said, "is the unity of word and deed. Lenin's entire merit consists in his will to carry out his program. . . . Land to the peasants, factories to the working class, power to those who toil. These words have often been spoken, but no one has ever thought seriously of passing from theory to practice. Lenin seems to be on the way. . . . "

"You mean," said Segui, bantering and incredulous, "that socialists are going to apply their program? Such a thing has never been seen. . . . "

I explained that just this was going to happen in Russia. It required all the ignorance and frivolity of the Western press to imagine that the Russian Revolution could be stabilized on the basis of democratic half-measures, while widespread misery, intensified by the most brutal repression, put before the Russian people all the basic problems: land, peace, power. An inexorable logic drove thousands of men into action, but they needed a clear conception of methods and aims. Would they achieve it? That was the question. The masses do not always at the decisive moment find men capable of expressing

9

unflinchingly their interests, their aspirations, and their latent power. The cultured classes, that is to say, the propertied classes, have plenty of representatives, plenty of conscientious guides, and good servants — nor do they hesitate to draw them from the common people if that becomes necessary. The poorer classes are poor in men and that is one of their greatest tragedies. The Paris Commune of 1871 carried on its struggle under incompetent leadership, groping and divided, while Blanqui,[1] the only mind who might have thought clearly for the revolutionists, was shut up in the dungeons of the Taureau. If in 1932 the German working class had had at its disposal the firm intelligence of a Rosa Luxemburg[2] and the revolutionary passion of a Karl Liebknecht,[3] would it have capitulated without a struggle to the rising wave of Nazism? Would we have witnessed the countless retreats of the Social Democracy and the pitiful maneuvers of the communists?

There are times when a people needs only a man and some men. . . . I advisedly say "one and some," for the former is nothing if not backed up by an active group which has faith in him and in which he has faith: in other words, a party. Given a party, an intellect, a will, history will be made.* But if society does not have these elements of crystallization, nothing will happen; reformism will land the revolution up a blind alley, and much blood will flow in vain. Throughout Europe the revolutions of 1848 were abortive. More recently certain ephemeral mystiques have arisen — to use a fashionable, rather meaningless word — on the one hand, the mystique of the plan, on the other, the mystique of the leader and of violence. And the plan remains a plan, the leader is deflated, and glorified violence turns into a cafe brawl. . . .

In its beginnings the Russian Revolution was at once grandiose in its inner necessity and pitiful in its outer helplessness. On the very day when the textile workers of Petrograd launched the strikes which less than a month later led to the downfall of absolutism, the Bolshevik Committee of one district of the capital advised against the strike. Just as the troops were about to mutiny — and it was this mutiny that brought about the downfall of the empire — those same revolutionists were timorously considering whether to advise a return to work. The

---

*A trade-union confederation may conceivably play the same role; or an alliance, a front, or a bloc, although the heterogeneity of these formations is a cause of weakness. It is wise to attach more importance to realities than to words. The anarchist FAI (**Federacion Anarquista Iberica**), in Spain has always claimed not to be a party, but it is one in the most effective sense of the word. — V. S.

revolutionists of every party, who had spent their entire life preparing for the revolution, did not realize that it was at hand, that the victory had already begun. Caught in the stream of events, they moved with the crowds, according to the mood of the moment. Suddenly, there was no longer an empire, no longer a ministry, no longer a czar. The minister of the interior, a septuagenarian with a quivering lower lip, met a socialist he thought he recognized in a hall of the Tauride Palace, and caught him by the sleeve, "What can I do for you, sir?" asked the socialist. "I am Protopopov. I beseech you, have me arrested. . . . "

The bourgeoisie itself, not numerous in Russia, and due to its economic situation very much aloof from the masses of the people, had politically ceased to exist. If at that time (February, old Russian calendar; it was March according to the western calendar), a Lenin or a Trotsky had been present at the first Council of the Workers and Soldiers, at the first soviet which was chaotically formed in the subcommittee rooms of the Duma — a clear mind gifted with the extraordinary audacity which one must have during periods of great turmoil to see things as they are and to draw the necessary inferences — Russia might have been able to economize by having only one revolution. The power of the soviets was the center of everything. There was then no other. One hundred and fifty thousand men in arms, the whole garrison, and more than half a million workers, listened to no other voice than that of their Soviet of Deputies. . . . But their only spokesmen were the socialists of the three influential parties, the Social Revolutionaries, the Menshevik-Social Democrats, and the Bolshevik-Social Democrats, all equally moderate, that is to say, frightened and incapable of controlling events by force of intelligence.

The negotiations regarding the question of power were farcical despite the grandeur of the moment. All the socialists had but one concern: to abdicate. At two o'clock in the afternoon of February 27 — when the downfall of the old regime was already irrevocable — Miliukov, the most able politician of the liberal bourgeoisie, thought that "it is still too soon" to form a provisional government, for no one can tell which way things may turn. Let us wait and observe. The bourgeoisie abdicated in the face of the tempest. On the first of March, the newly formed Executive Committee of the Soviet asked the bourgeoisie to form a government without even stipulating a program. Essentially eager to abdicate, the socialists asked nothing more for themselves than freedom of propaganda; quite a new thing, it is true, throughout Russia and Siberia. . . .

An example of disinterestedness for all peoples and ages! Socialists, having all the power in their hands, and upon whom alone it depended whether freedom of agitation should be given to others or not, handed over the power to their "class enemy" upon the condition that the latter should promise them . . . freedom of agitation! Rodzianko was afraid to go to the telegraph office and said to Chkheidze and Sukhanov: "You have the power, you can arrest us all." Chkheidze and Sukhanov answered him: "Take the power, but don't arrest us for propaganda." . . . Fearing, nevertheless, that the bourgeoisie might not agree to take the power on the proposed conditions, Sukhanov delivered a threatening ultimatum: "Either we or nobody can control the elements . . . there is but one way out—agree to our terms." In other words: accept the program, which is your program; for this we promise to subdue for you the masses who gave us the power. Poor subduers of the elements! [4]

The liberals gave in to this gentle violence and formed the Provisional Government. They still hoped to cede power in their turn to the monarchy, insisting only that it be constitutional. They tried to save the dynasty. There was a contest to see who could do the most abdicating: Nicholas II abdicated in favor of Grand Duke Michael; the Grand Duke, in favor of a problematical constituent assembly. . . .

THE REVOLUTION FINDS A MAN

Thus the Russian Revolution occurred spontaneously; at the beginning it seemed to have no one to help it along. And a great lesson may be drawn from this: such events can neither be hastened nor precipitated. Anyone is blind who imagines that he can be for or against historical necessity. But if men who distinguish its real features put themselves at its service, they will enable it to yield the greatest possible harvest; and the better they are able to integrate themselves into the inexorable course of events and consciously derive their underlying laws, the more they will be able to achieve. Only such men can be revolutionists — and it is a matter of no consequence that many of them are by personal predilection the most peace-

---

*Sukhanov's memoirs give a detailed account of these negotiations. In 1931 Sukhanov was sentenced to thirty years' imprisonment in Moscow for forming a socialist group. — V. S.

ful of bookworms. When the moment comes, they leave the libraries to pile paving stones on the barricades, to assist the section committees with their advice. Until Lenin's arrival in Russia, the revolution marked time.

The year 1917 was the fourth year of the World War. For a thousand days every able-bodied man in all the great countries of Europe had been in uniform. The flower of the youth of a continent, an entire generation of young men were mowed down. Thirty million men had been mobilized. It was the epoch of the cannon. Europe was traversed by battle lines, from the North Sea to the Adriatic, from the Baltic to the Mediterranean. Along these blood-soaked frontiers, thousands of combatants died each day. It was a war of trenches, mines, tanks, airplanes, gas, submarines, and poisonous lies. At the front, soldiers met their death by their "own" firing squads or on the enemy barbed wire; behind the lines men trafficked in their blood and steeped themselves in insipid military communiques.

The year 1917 was in France the year of Clemenceauism, of General Nivelle, and the offensive of April 16. The "breakthrough" at the Chemin des Dames. The useless battles of Flanders and Verdun, the drive of the tanks at Cambrai. Serbia, the north of France, Belgium, and Poland were heaps of corpses. Germany declared unrestricted submarine warfare against England. Merchant vessels were torpedoed, neutrals were drowned. Death stalked the seas.

There was fighting in Macedonia, Mesopotamia, Palestine, in the distant corners of the African Bush. The United States entered the war. Blacks, Hindus, Australians, Canadians, Portuguese were in arms; the blood of all races flowed into one pool and one stench. America milked the belligerents of all the gold they had left.

The Central Powers broke through the Italian Front at Caporetto; the Germans and Austrians drove toward the Piave. Zeppelins over London. Gothas over Paris. Gothas over Venice. French planes over Stuttgart. Air aces on both sides downed their fiftieth enemy plane. Parades, decorations.

Behind the lines, the cannon and munition manufacturers of both sides coined profits. Martial law, censorship. Women and old men in anguish. Appalling poverty, debauchery, the bread card, the coal card; all humanity at the mercy of stupidity and hatred. Conscientious objectors were persecuted in Great Britain, defeatists in France, internationalists everywhere. Churches, political parties, intellectuals, both in the Central Powers and in the Allied camp, preached war to the bitter end. Wartime socialism was introduced on both sides. The whole of science and technology was used to destroy the living strength of the human species and the achievements of civilization. Employed rationally, the wealth that was dissipated in explosives would have amply sufficed — if we may speak in Utopian terms — to give ease and comfort to all in a renovated society.

It was the fourth year of the war for the partitioning of the globe among the financial imperialists.[5]

Suddenly, in that black year, the crash of an empire drowns out the sound of the cannon. The Russian people demand peace for all the peoples, land to the peasants, the factories to the workers. The Russian people is in arms, for the war has given them guns. This people has more deaths behind it than any other. More oppression, more misery. This people is capable of anything. Will it have the necessary audacity of will? Will it achieve consciousness of its strength?

On April 3, 1917, Lenin arrived at the Finland Station in Petrograd. With him came Gregory Zinoviev and others. He was almost an unknown — N. Lenin, V. I. Ulyanov. The man was forty-seven years old, and already had a revolutionary past of thirty years duration. In his youth, the shadow of the gallows had crossed his life; the executioner of Czar Alexander III had hanged his elder brother. At twenty-three, he founded in St. Petersburg one of the first Russian Marxist groups. He spent several years in exile in Siberia. By 1913 he had become known to the leaders of the Russian labor movement as an uncompromising doctrinaire (through the formation of the *Iskra* — Spark — and the split of the Social Democratic Labor Party of Russia into the intransigent Bolsheviks, or the revolutionary majority, and the Mensheviks, the opportunist minority). As an emigre in London, Paris, Switzerland, Finland, and Cracow, scarcely known outside of his party, he had worked untiringly at his proudly proclaimed "trade" — of theoretician, propagandist, and organizer of the proletariat — in a word, of revolutionist. His party of intransigents — whom the Socialist International pleased to call "fanatics" — formed, or rather forged, by him, had unlimited faith in him. He had directed this party wisely during one revolution (1905). He was much talked of in political circles, as were his writings on materialist philosophy and political economy; he was a scholar. The minutes of International Socialist Congresses mention his activity; journalists, on the lookout for celebrities, never even noticed his presence. At

Stuttgart in 1907, where Lenin supported Rosa Luxemburg, Herve[6] was very much in the limelight; Lenin passed unnoticed. But at the time of the greatest betrayals in August 1914, when the majority of the celebrities of socialism, syndicalism, anarchism, suddenly became converted to support of the war, Lenin — sure of the future when everything seemed lost for the labor movement, which was enslaved to delirious patriotism — Lenin began, stone by stone, to lay the foundations of the Third International. At Zimmerwald[7] in 1915, internationalists were terrified to hear him talk calmly of revolution.

In the fourth year of the war, this man left his Zurich home with calm determination. Months later he was "the most hated and most loved man on earth." With unflagging intelligence and firmness, he directed the first social revolution of modern times.

In that dusk of civilization, he brought the proletariat a new reason for living.

To conquer.[8]

He said, "The war has for its aim a new partition of the world among the Great Powers, dominated by the financial oligarchies."

"Change the imperialist war into a civil war."

"Form a new Socialist International which will be an International of revolutionary action."

He saw plainly the limits of the possible, but he meant to exhaust these limits. He did not proclaim socialism in Russia, but the expropriation of the big estates for the benefit of the peasants; workers' control over production; a democratic dictatorship of the toilers, with the hegemony of the working class at its core.

Hardly off the train, he asked the party comrades, "Why didn't you seize power?"

And at once he comes out with his April Theses, outlining the program for the seizure of power. He is called mad, delirious. He smiles maliciously, sits down at a finely wrought desk in the palace of one of the Czar's favorites, and begins once again to write. The experienced militants censure him; *Pravda* disavows him. But suddenly it becomes apparent that he has the ear of the man in the street, and of the man in the factory and barracks! His whole genius consists only in his ability to say what these people want to say, but do not know how to say — in his ability to say what no politician or revolutionist has until now succeeded in saying.

In three weeks, without a struggle, he had a majority in the party; it was no longer a question of fusing with reformists and attempting to stabilize the parliamentary republic.

"The party wants a more democratic proletarian and peasant republic, in which the police and the standing army will be replaced by the armed people."[9]

The party wanted a "people's autocracy," in which the people had the right to elect and recall functionaries; in which the legislative and executive powers were united in the councils of workers' and soldiers' deputies (soviets); "the right of all nations to self-determination"; "nationalization of banks, trusts, and cartels"; confiscation of the land to be immediately turned over to the peasants organized in soviets; a general peace, which was to be "a workers' peace, directed against all the capitalists."

There was nothing in the program which could not be carried out; on the contrary, it would have been difficult and dangerous at this time not to carry it out. But force and courage were required to insure its success; it was necessary to break with theoretical inertia, and to break with powerful interests. Many men were making a living out of the war, and Russia was tied to her allies. The propertied classes, threatened with the loss of everything, would defend themselves; despite their weakness, they would put up some very serious resistance. Their challenge must be accepted. Lenin's merit consisted in being a revolutionist in time of revolution.

THE SECOND HEAD OF A REVOLUTION

When an idea is in the air of an epoch, that is to say, when the general conditions for its birth and growth are present, men begin to have a presentiment of it, and it is frequently conceived by several men at the same time. This is how the truth of a period comes to fruition. It is true of the sciences as well as of politics, which is in some ways a science and an art at the same time. Darwin and Wallace discovered almost simultaneously the theory of natural selection, suggested no doubt by the aspect of the young capitalist society then in full process of development. Joule and Meyer discovered the law of the conservation of energy almost simultaneously. Marx and Engels arrived at the same conclusion as to the foundations of modern society and, in twenty-five years of admirable intellectual collaboration, founded scientific socialism. The Russian Revolution was to realize in action—but action nourished by solid thought—a collaboration just as remarkable: that of Lenin and Trotsky.

Expelled from France in 1916 by an order signed by Malvy (Jules Guesde was in the cabinet), [10] as a result of a provocation; then deported from Spain as an undesirable element, Trotsky went to New York, where he stayed for a short time, engaged in revolutionary activity; and then to Canada whence he planned to set sail for Russia. Interned in a concentration camp with his wife and children, he finally was set free, thanks to the intervention of the Petrograd Soviet. He arrived in the capital on May 5, 1917, and his first speech, delivered as soon as he got off the boat, demanded the seizure of power. His personality as an orator, journalist, and organizer sometimes seemed to overshadow that of Lenin, which at first glance appeared less striking. Lenin was good-natured, unassuming, ordinary in appearance; an outsider would scarcely have noticed him; he spoke with extreme simplicity, and it was not so much his language as the force of his reasoning which moved his audience. He wrote, without particular gift or concern for form, what he had to say and nothing more. Never in his life did he make the slightest concession to the demon of literature. Trotsky, on the other hand, would nowhere have passed unnoticed, with his shock of hair, the erect carriage of his head, the intensity of his blue-gray eyes. He had about him something authorative and compelling. On the platform his voice had a metallic ring, and each sentence was like a sharp thrust. He was to become the orator par excellence of this revolution. His written style was consummately skillful. But the main thing was that the hour which had struck was the hour he had awaited, foreseen, and desired all his life. In the Social Democratic Party he was the theoretician of the permanent revolution, which means a revolution which cannot and will not be extinguished before it has completed its work, and which consequently can be conceived only on an international plane.

By his knowledge of languages and peoples, he was the most European of the Russian revolutionists. Lenin had, however, one incontestable superiority over him: his party—formed through fourteen years of struggles and labors, from 1903 to 1917. We have seen how this party changed its state of mind and its program after Lenin's arrival in Russia; it might be said to have arrived at conceptions which had for a long time been familiar to Trotsky, yet Trotsky and his group entered

it. The documents of the period were for years not to separate
the names of these two men who, by and large, thought and
acted as one, translating the thought and action of millions.
These were the two heads of the revolution. Upon them was
concentrated all the popularity, and they bore all the hatred.
Every day Maxim Gorky in his *Novaya Zhizn* denounced
these two criminal fomenters of anarchy:

> Lenin, Trotsky, and their cohorts are already intoxicated
> with the poison of power, as is proved by their shameful
> attitude toward freedom of speech, personal liberty and
> that group of rights for which democracy has struggled. . . .
> Lenin and his acolytes believe themselves entitled to com-
> mit every crime. . . .
> Lenin is not an all-powerful magician, but a cynical
> sleight-of-hand performer who cares neither for honor nor
> for the life of the proletariat. . . .
> Vladimir   Lenin   is   introducing   a   socialist   regime
> in   Russia . . . full   steam   ahead   into   the   mire. Lenin,
> Trotsky, and all those who with them are headed for ruin
> in the quagmire of reality, are apparently convinced that
> a Russian can best be led by holding out to him the right
> to disgrace himself. . . .

Thus wrote Maxim Gorky in 1917. [11]
When, at the beginning of the civil war, the Social Revolutionaries considered killing the leaders of Bolshevism, they
had these two in mind. They shot at Lenin and wounded him;
bombs were planted to blow up Trotsky's train. Terrorists
sought to ambush him at a railroad station; by the purest
chance he took another route. The documents and writings
of the period infallibly place these two collaborators at the
heart or at the peak of the events. Jacques Sadoul's *Notes
sur la Revolution Bolchevique*, John Reed's *Ten Days that
Shook the World*, Guilbeaux's *Portrait authentique de Lenine*
give valuable accounts of the period. In 1923, Andre Morizet,
just back from Moscow, wrote a book and called it *Chez Lenine
et Trotski*. "Trotsky," wrote Sadoul to Albert Thomas, "domi-
nates the insurrection. He is its soul of steel, while Lenin is
its theoretician." [12]
The Provisional Government, having in June 1917 launched
vast offensives on all fronts — at the urgent demand of the
Allies, whose sole concern was to relieve the Western front
at all costs — suddenly found itself confronted by disaster. Its

shock battalions were cut to pieces by machine guns, the main bodies of troops disbanded. It was of no avail to flog the soldiers (it had come to that), or shoot them, for whole regiments simply melted away in the summer's heat. Men left the front, carrying their guns and ammunition along with them, demanding that peace be concluded. The garrison and the factories of Petrograd went out into the streets, urged on by the anarchists, but against the advice of the Bolsheviks, who felt that the country was not yet ripe for the seizure of power. Kerensky could count on loyal Cossacks in sufficient number to quell the disturbance. The next day the Bolsheviks were outlawed. Lenin and Zinoviev hid in a hut near the Baltic Sea, in Finland, where Lenin wrote his work on the state. Trotsky allowed himself to be arrested, at the risk of being murdered or executed, so that at least one of the two should openly proclaim his responsibility.

At this point a poison for use against them was discovered, a most effective kind of poison, which failed only by a hair's breadth in killing them and the nascent revolution with them.

SLANDER, A STRONG POISON

During the night of July 4, 1917, a mysterious rumor spread through the corridors of the Soviet. Proofs had been discovered of the treason of Lenin and Trotsky. Irrefutable documents, stolen from the German General Staff, were to be published. Telegrams in code. Signed receipts. They had received millions!

The press of the whole world ran the news in banner headlines: *the Bolsheviks are paid agents of Germany!*

The threads of intrigue led to Stockholm, where there was a German espionage agency. Kerensky felt that "facts of extreme importance" had been unearthed. A letter had been published — seized in the mail somewhere, it seemed — in which a German Baron "congratulated the Bolsheviks on their work," and predicted "the joy that would be felt in Berlin." It was recalled that Lenin, Zinoviev, and a dozen other Russian socialists had reached Russia by crossing Germany in wartime — in a "sealed railway car." (In Germany, Lenin had refused to see anyone, and especially the social democrats. . . . "Liebknecht, yes," he said, "and gladly.") The liberal Minister, Paul Miliukov, spoke of the role of German gold in the Russian Revolution. An

investigation was started which history did not permit to be
completed or even to be formally discontinued. Events were
moving too fast. A former agent of the Russian counterespionage service, after having informed us that "the agents in
the course of their investigations manufactured their own documents," later came to the rather startling conclusion that not
only the Bolsheviks but the anti-Bolsheviks as well were guilty
of treason. In his opinion, the only ones not guilty of treason
were the counterespionage agents; they simply spent their time
manufacturing documents of a treasonous nature. . . .

"The counterespionage reports on Lenin's previous activity,"
wrote this Mr. Ustinov, "on his connections with the German
General Staff, and on the fact that he had received German
gold, were so convincing that he should have been hanged at
once."

Kerensky did not do anything about this, however, since he
himself was a "well-known" traitor.

If I mention these facts, it is because slander, throughout
the Russian Revolution, has had a curious history, and because it has today reappeared in identical form. The legend
of the German gold rapidly died down in 1917 — and slander
played no part in the social struggles of the epic years; it was
not to reappear until ten years later, in 1927-1928. But from
then on it soared to dizzy heights.

THE MARCH TO POWER

In September 1917, General Kornilov's putsch collapsed piti-
fully, and the situation was completely transformed. Reality,
stronger than slanderous legends based on facsimiles forged
in the offices of the secret service, showed who the revolutionists
were and who were the phrase-mongers, fakers, and counterrevolutionists. The Kerensky cabinet demonstrated clearly that it
was nothing more than a phantom government, buffeted about
between two possible dictatorships: either the generals, who on
the reactionary side were the only men gifted with sufficient insight and force (for in periods of social instability any military
second-rater is intelligent enough to comprehend the benefits,
to the financiers, of authority), would resume their activity
and the revolution would go the way of Bonapartism; or else

the workers, soldiers, and peasants, the Soviets, the Bolsheviks, would conquer by force, since there was no other way. What compromise could there be between military dictatorship and proletarian dictatorship?

Lenin and Trotsky see this plainly and hence they demand, suggest, proclaim, and initiate the advance toward insurrection. The one, at the head of the party, which he succeeds in convincing not without resistance; the other, at the head of the Petrograd Soviet where he forms a Revolutionary Military Committee, distributes arms to the workers, and persuades the Soviet to decide that the revolutionary garrison will not obey the Provisional Government and will not leave the city. He has organized the insurrection before the actual uprising.

In their private conversations these two men sometimes expressed concern. They felt themselves too indispensable.

"If we are killed," asked Lenin of Trotsky, "do you think Bukharin and Sverdlov will manage?"

I once drew this portrait of them. Though it was written in 1919, I see no reason to modify a single line of it.

The experts are gone. Two men remain at the center of the Supreme Council.

With its careworn faces, and papers covered with specialists' figures, the Council resembles the directors' meeting of a firm that is terribly in the red. Debit: the White terror in Budapest, the defeat in Hamburg, the silence of Berlin, the silence in Paris, the vacillations of Jean Longuet, the loss of Orel, the threat to Tula. More debit: that yesterday we were nothing; that we have arisen from poverty, from darkness, from continuous defeat. Credit: the news from Italy, the strikes in Turin, the rivalry between Washington and Tokyo, the statements of Serrati and of Pierre Brizon. Credit: the consciousness, the will, the blood of the proletarians. Further: the frightful liabilities of a civilization bearing the ulcer of war in its flesh. And propaganda has transferred the 11,000 assassinated by the White terror in Finland to the credit side. . . .

At the moment, amid the silence of the toiling masses, the entire struggle is embodied in these two leaders. It is they whose wearisome effigies are everywhere to be seen; in homes, offices, and clubs; in the papers and in the displays of sycophant photographers who vie with one another for the honor of snapping their pictures. Once, when they were in good spirits, after a great success in the nationalization of the coal mines, they exchanged an ironic remark or

two on the subject of the new icons. "Look at all
the portraits! Don't you think they're going too far?" "The
drawbacks of popularity, my friend, are the sycophants
and imbeciles who puff it up." Both of them were sarcastic
but there the resemblance ended: the one, good-natured with
a large, bald forehead, rather prominent cheekbones, a
prominent nose, a wisp of reddish beard, a striking air
of health, simplicity, sly intelligence. When he laughed, his
eyes narrowed and sparkled green. He had an enormous
prominent forehead, a big mouth, a jovial expression re-
vealing Asiatic traits mingled with the European. . . .

The other was a Jew. At times he had about him the force-
ful ugliness of an eagle; in his glance there was piercing
intelligence. He carried his head like a leader of men; and
had an air of inner certainty that shortsighted observers
might have taken for pride; his laugh was a Mephisto-
phelian mask — and in it there was something misleading —
for this man retained the capacity for joy of a young man
with all life's struggles ahead of him.

They laughed at their own portraits. "I only hope," said
one, "that we live long enough to make them stop printing
these." "I hope," said the other, "that we live long enough
not to be canonized"* [13]

But they were not leaders in the sense that this word has
assumed   since   the   appearance   of   the   Duce,   the   Ghazi,
the Fuehrer, and the Beloved Leader in the USSR. Their popularity was not manufactured nor imposed; it grew up spontaneously on the basis of the confidence they earned. Their
actions and their words were discussed everywhere. And more
than that. They answered their enemies with a shrug of the
shoulders; to the workers they explained their position and
sometimes found themselves outvoted. They were only the first
among comrades, and they would have accorded a cold reception to the dangerous imbecile who took it into his head
to place them above their comrades or above the party. The
life of the Politbureau and the Central Committee was at all
times collective. The party discussed, tendencies appeared and
disappeared, and opposition elements, which must not be confused with counterrevolutionists, agitated unceasingly in broad
daylight during the whole civil war — until 1921. They were not
to disappear completely until 1925-1926, when in consequence

*Writing these words at Leningrad, I could not use the names.
If I had, the Black Chamber would not have passed my manuscript. — V. S.

all internal life disappeared from the party. Lenin invited old opponents, Martov and Dan, the Menshevik leaders, to speak in the Central Executive Committee of the Soviets. Anarchists belonged to the committee. The Left Social Revolutionaries participated in the power for several months at the beginning of the regime. They were eliminated only after having attempted an uprising and fired cannon in the very streets of Moscow in July 1918. No one thought of fighting for a totalitarian state; men fought and died for a new kind of freedom. Bolshevism triumphed by proclaiming to the masses and to the world a democracy of free workers, such as had never before been seen. The first Soviet Constitution drawn up by Sverdlov guaranteed every liberty to the toilers. No one, for example, thought of abolishing the freedom of the press the day after the victorious insurrection. The Bolsheviks' aim was "to take the monopoly of the press from the bourgeoisie." With this end in view it was necessary to suppress the reactionary press which, moreover, specialized in campaigns of slander. But, said Trotsky, "every group of citizens should have printing presses and paper at their disposal." And Lenin put forth a proposal that every group of citizens supported by 10,000 to 15,000 toilers should have the right to issue a paper if it wished.

THE VICTORY OF NOVEMBER 7, 1917

We cannot overemphasize the fact that in the course of the last ten years, the words "leaders," "parties," "Soviets," "masses," have altogether changed their meaning, and have come to signify the exact opposite of what they meant during the great years of hope and victory. The whole history of the early days has had to be laboriously made over, and the process is not yet completed. At the time of the November insurrection, the leaders were only the foremost, the most respected and most authoritative of the militants; the Bolshevik Party was the political organization which best expressed the popular sentiment. From this fact came its popularity and the effectiveness of its activity.

With the aid of some little-known texts, we shall try to give a general picture of their activity during the decisive days.

Bukharin tells us in a document which appeared in 1922:

It was in Petersburg during the Democratic Conference.

Try to visualize the Winter Palace; Kerensky was there, just back from Moscow after the unfortunate experiment of a government conference in that city, where the workers received him by calling a strike so general that the waiters at the Hotel Metropole refused even to wait on the delegates. . . . But first I want to tell a little story about our party life at that time, which is still half a secret. Lenin was in hiding. Immediately before the Democratic Conference convoked by Kerensky, our Central Committee met. Our tactics were perfectly clear. Agitation and propaganda among the masses and preparation for the insurrection which was imminent. I had no sooner come in than Miliutin came up to me and said: "Comrade Bukharin, we've just received a little note."

This note said: "You are scoundrels and traitors if you do not immediately send Bolsheviks into the mills and factories, and if you do not have the rascals in the Democratic Conference surrounded and arrested." The whole letter was written in that style and was full of threats. We were all amazed; no one up to that time had dared to bring up the question so bluntly. No one knew what to do. Finally a decision was taken. This was perhaps the only time in the history of our party that the Central Committee unanimously decided to burn a letter from Lenin. The affair was never made public. At that time we were to the right of Lenin who, as you see, is not always for moderation and timeliness and is capable of wide swings to the left, and of being mistaken. . . . We rejected his demands because we felt that though we were unquestionably able to take over Moscow and Petrograd and to dissolve the Democratic Conference, we could, nevertheless, not maintain ourselves in power throughout the rest of Russia. But at the Conference I saw a characteristic little scene which showed up clearly the general state of mind. After Kerensky, Trotsky took the floor. Kerensky's group was surrounded by sailors whom Kerensky had brought there to protect the Democratic Conference against a Bolshevik coup. I saw Trotsky come down from the platform after his speech, and together we went over among the sailors who started to wave their bayonets and ask Trotsky whether it would not soon be time to make use of them. The few troops of the Provisional Government were already on our side.

This was in the middle of September. Six weeks later, the

day of the Second Congress of the Soviets, the insurrection broke out. In Petrograd it triumphed easily, in Moscow at the cost of much suffering and bloodshed. In several places there had been spontaneous uprisings before this date, notably in Kazan and in Tashkent, where the soviets and the troops had not waited for instructions. For some time Kronstadt and the Baltic Fleet had obeyed no one but themselves. Kronstadt was strongly under the influence of the Bolsheviks and anarchists; the Navy obeyed the directives of the party.

Antonov-Ovseenko, today Soviet consul general in Barcelona, tells the following story of the capture of the Winter Palace:

I drive to the local military headquarters at top speed. We pass our sentries in Millionaya Street; there is disorganized firing around the palace, several soldiers have just surrendered. Darkness. Shots ring out. The chatter of machine guns. A crowd of sailors, soldiers, and Red Guards rush up the street and then retreat, hugging the walls when the cadets open fire from behind their log barricades. Finally the cannons utter a muffled roar. Again and again. That is the Peter Paul fortress (situated on the other side of the Neva). "Shouldn't we ask them to surrender?" suggests Chudnovsky, who has just arrived at the head of some men from the Pavlovsky regiment. He is bold and loquacious as usual. I agree. The sound of the cannon has had its effect. The Woman's Battalion starts to weep, and cries out that they will never do it again. The military school surrenders; the cadets lay their guns on the sidewalk in bundles and leave under escort. Chudnovsky wants to let them keep their guns, but I won't allow it. Other cadets resisted for an hour longer. It was hard to attack them, the only approach being a narrow, winding stairway. Several times they forced the crowd back. At length, however, they weakened and sent a message that they were giving up all resistance. With Chudnovsky I went up into the apartments of the palace. The remains of barricades, mattresses, arms, cartridge cases, crusts of bread were scattered everywhere. A motley crowd rushed up after us. We invaded the upper floors; the cadets surrendered. Suddenly we found ourselves in a vast hall, before a door guarded by a row of young people with rifles crossed. They hesitate for a moment. Chudnovsky and I approach this last defense of the Provisional Government. They seemed petrified. We had difficutly tearing

their rifles from their grasp. "Is the Provisional Government here?" "It is here," one of the cadets replies obsequi-
ously. And then he whispers: "I am with you." This is the
last bourgeois government of old Russia. These thirteen
men — for Kerensky had fled that morning "to summon
help" — were no more than wan shadows sitting around
a table. We arrest them. The crowd wants to kill them
on the spot, but we escort them safely to the Peter Paul
fortress.

On board the cruiser *Aurora,* anchored in the Neva several
hundred yards away, revolutionists were awaiting the order
to open fire in earnest (they had already fired some blanks)
on the Palace.

We were about to give a last order which might have
been fatal both for the ministers of the "democracy" and
for the Palace. We decided to wait another quarter of an
hour, feeling instinctively that the situation might change.
We were not mistaken. The last few minutes were ticking
away when a new messenger arrived straight from the
Winter Palace. "The Palace has been taken." This time our
rejoicing was double, because we had been on the point
of opening fire, and this unknown sailor — no one bothered
to identify him — had saved the Palace.
With a friend of mine, I immediately drove to Smolny.
Our sailors had procured the car. They had just taken
five autos from bourgeois and functionaries in the vicinity.
The streets of Petersburg were calm and silent. Not a
sign of insurrection. Revolutionary sentries warmed themselves around bonfires at street intersections. They let us
by without any trouble. We even saw crowded street cars
with their lights on. In a word, there was not a trace of
revolution. At Smolny the delegates of the Congress were
leaving their meeting after the first session of the Executive Committee of the Soviet Republic, which had been
formed with astounding rapidity. It was all over. I went
back on board and went to bed.
The next day we decided to purify the atmosphere a
bit, by showing the bourgeois rabble our revolutionary
bayonets. Patrols of sailors set out for the center of town
with orders to disperse any crowds. They did succeed in
calming the general effervescence. They usually brought
back trophies of revolvers, sabres, rifles, and even bombs;
they also brought in suspects: officers, drunks, gentlemen

excessively bourgeois in appearance, soldiers of the shock battalions. They were all treated with the greatest forbearance: after a brief questioning, they were dismissed. The soldiers were advised, amid great gaiety, to go back to their apron strings; the drunks were given jam to eat and then sent upstairs to sleep. This friendly reception soon caused the building to be full of drunks. Thereupon the sailors thought up another method which in the autumn season was quite drastic, and that was to dip the drunks in the river. That sobered them up immediately, and we were soon rid of them. (Reminiscences of Flerovsky).

On October 26 (November 8) Jacques Sadoul wrote to the deputy Albert Thomas in Champigny-sur-Marne:

My dear Thomas: This is the day of the insurrection. This morning on my way to the Mission, I saw the corpse of General Tumanov, an adjunct in the War Ministry, fished out of the Moika. The soldiers arrested him last night and killed him with their bayonets. Amid laughter they placed him on a low cart in a ridiculous pose and led him off to the morgue. The news is good for the Bolsheviks. The Winter Palace was bombarded, then pillaged. All the works of art, tapestries, paintings were savagely destroyed. The Woman's Battalion, which defended it, was taken prisoner and shut up in a barracks, where the poor girls are said to have been raped as much as anyone can be.

Many of them are young women of the bourgeoisie. Most of the members of the Provisional Government were arrested. Kerensky fled. The army is in the hands of the revolutionists.

All that Sadoul says on the pillage of the Winter Palace is false. Perhaps a few women soldiers were not treated with all the respect due to a disarmed enemy. But on the whole, there were practically no excesses. From the same letter:

Again I see the great leaders. I make the acquaintance of Lenin and Trotsky.

. . . Interlude at one o'clock in the morning. I interview Trotsky at length. A few minutes later he is elected Minister, or rather People's Commissar of Foreign Affairs.

First question: his opinion on the insurrection.

"Every revolution has its hazards, but the chances of

success are enormous. The preparations were made with
the greatest care. The organization extends over the whole
Russian territory, and a thousand committees have been
set up: almost the entire army has been won over. The
peasant masses will be won over by the division of the
estates of the big landowners. Based on these two elements,
the movement must succeed. One sweep of the broom was
sufficient to drive out the weak-kneed mediocrities of the
former government." [14]

In Moscow the street battles lasted for six days. There were
terrible episodes such as the massacre of the workers of the
Kremlin arsenal by the defenders of the democratic order.
Before the insurrection, Muralov had undertaken the study
of insurrectional technique. He was an agronomist, a fine
giant of a Bolshevik. As early as February he had had the
splendid idea of occupying the public buildings with a few
companies of soldiers, and this brought about the fall of
czarism in the old capital. He writes:

> I looked for a pamphlet put out by our party in 1905
> on the tactics of street fighting, but I did not find it. It
> had disappeared in the course of a house-to-house search.
> So I was obliged to rely on my memory. In addition I
> tried to lead some officers I knew to these topics of con-
> versation.

Muralov fought like a fiend. At the moment when everything
seemed lost for the Soviet fighters:

> . . . the artillery joined our infantry, and we regained
> courage. I no longer remember how many cannon there
> were, but Vladimir Smirnov, the commander of our artillery,
> must remember. . . .

In the notes of Vladimir Smirnov I find a dynamic page
on this subject:

> When I informed the soldiers that we were surrounded
> and that the Revolutionary Committee instructed them to
> retreat (It was night. They were sleeping, utterly tired out.),
> they replied calmly: "We are staying."
> The next day we attacked in one place with a certain
> success, and this encouraged us; the following day a group
> of our people occupied the tower of the Strastnaya monastery,

where the cadets had ensconced themselves with a machine gun. That night I was sent with two comrades to the Khodynka artillery brigade, and we brought back two or three cannon, one of which we set up in Strastnaya Square to fire on the mansion of the former Governor General. A few shells were sufficient to dislodge a corps of students. When they were conducted to the soviets, it took considerable effort to persuade the soldiers of the guard not to shoot them. The Revolutionary Committee then decided on a general attack, and I was commissioned to ask the Fifty-fifth Infantry for reinforcements. We set out in a closed Red Cross car. We were stopped en route by students of the officers' training school and taken to Alexander High School in Arbat. They began to search us. Recognizing me, a young officer of the Fifty-fifth tore off my tunic, crying out that I was a Bolshevik and that I should be stood up against the wall. I passed one or two nights there, and then one evening a cannon boomed, and they marched us out, about eighty to a hundred prisoners. An escort of students marched us to the Kremlin. The leader of the escort, one Prince Trubetskoy, told the soldiers to "jab a bayonet into the back of anyone who dared to turn his head." At the Kremlin the officers received us with insults. One of them cried out: "Either we're done for, or we'll beat this rabble." I passed the night in the barracks of the Fifty-fifth Regiment. Next evening a terrific explosion was heard: our artillery was firing on the Kremlin from the Mount of Sparrows. . . . The following day they marched about forty of us out, to shoot us we thought, but when we had reached the Nikolskaya gate, they had us pass before the sentinel and let us go. The Red Guards in front of St. Basil's church leveled their rifles at us, but we cried out that we were Reds. After that I went to the district soviet. They suggested that I take a little rest, and I ran to my home where I hadn't set foot for two weeks. I ate dinner and went to the Zamoskvoretchie headquarters. . . .

All this happened nineteen years ago. Muralov and Smirnov are living, and as I write these lines, I think of them with great emotion. In 1927 both sided with the party opposition against Stalin. Both were expelled from the party. Both were arrested. Vladimir Smirnov has been in prison ever since, except for a few days in 1932 when he was deported, re-arrested in exile, and handed another five year sentence — without known reasons. He had grown almost blind in his cell in

Suzdal. Where is he today? Nikolai Muralov was for a long time military governor of Moscow region. He was exiled to the forests of the Tara nearly eight years ago. In his exile he worked at his trade of agronomist. Recently he was arrested, accused of some fanciful plot, of high treason, intelligence with Hitler, and so on. He seems headed for the executioner.

THE GREAT YEARS

This is the beginning of the great years. I shall not attempt to describe all their alternating moments of despair and enthusiasm. I shall only indicate their principal dates and their general aspect. Immediately after the seizure of power the ministries were empty; functionaries, technicians, directors of factories, capitalists, and managers had in their turn discovered the strike and systematic sabotage. Red Guards, who were simply workers with a gun slung over their shoulder, sought out the leading functionaries of the ministries in their homes; a few were locked up, and others developed a certain degree of good will. . . . But the first months of this struggle went by with neither excesses nor terror. A counterrevolutionary effort in Petrograd and vicinity was easily broken by Trotsky, aided by Colonel Muraviev, who later turned traitor and was killed. Hardly anyone was arrested; and those who were were soon released. Among these were Krasnov, Ataman of the Cossacks, who took advantage of our leniency to start a civil war in the Don country — and Purishkievich, the anti-Semite leader. Lenin and his co-workers did not contemplate the total nationalization of heavy industry, but rather an effective workers' control and the growing participation of the socialist state in mixed trusts, in which the capitalists would retain some place.

The first question to be solved was that of the war. The soldiers were tired of fighting. "They are voting with their feet," said Lenin mockingly to those who wanted him to continue the war, a revolutionary war this time. "They are simply leaving the front." The Soviets proposed a general peace, but only the Central Powers consented to the opening of negotiations. General Dukhonin, who had refused to offer the enemy an armistice, was massacred by the sailors. (It since became a popular parlance to "send someone to Dukhonin's headquarters," meaning the hereafter. . . .) The Central Powers accepted in principle a peace without annexations and indemnities. But at the Brest-Litovsk negotiations Trotsky and Joffe, in the presence of Count Czernin, von Kuehlmann, and General Hoffman, were asked to sanction vast annexations under the name of "liberations." Thereupon they walked out and issued an appeal to the peoples themselves. The Soviets stopped the war, at the same time refusing to sign a shameful treaty. Trotsky had favored this solution as a means of feeling out the revolutionary possibilities in Germany; he thought that socially the enemy was no longer able to undertake an offensive against the Russian people. He was mistaken, though the Austrians were of the same opinion. William II put an end to the controversy by ordering an advance, whereupon Lenin forced through the Central Committee the decision to sign a less favorable peace, which sacrificed the revolution in Finland and the Ukraine. "We must sacrifice territory," he said, "in order to gain time." Sokolnikov, a member of the Central Committee, signed the treaty of Brest-Litovsk without taking the trouble to read it.

The Allies regarded this separate peace as a betrayal, although Lenin and Trotsky would have accepted the aid of France and England in defending the young Republic. "Accept arms from the imperialist bandits," Lenin scribbled on a piece of paper. In Russia the national sentiment, strong in the middle classes, was injured. This sentiment became a source of strength to us in the civil war.

The civil war began in the South by the formation of small national armies, known as White Armies, which rallied to the banner of the counterrevolution; the eastward movement of the Czechoslovak troops through the Volga regions gave the Allies the idea of using them to overthrow the Soviets in conjunction with the Social Revolutionaries. Various officers' plots followed in the big cities. A White insurrection gained the upper hand for a time in Yaroslav. The summer of 1918 was frightful. Famine, cholera in Petrograd, plots, assassinations, revolts of the Social Revolutionaries—who shared the power; Dora Kaplan fired several bullets into Lenin's chest as he was leaving a factory meeting. (And Lenin insisted that she should not be shot; although her execution was announced, I have reasons for believing that it did not take place and that Dora Kaplan was still alive many years later.) The Red terror then began; it was partly carried on by the People's Commissars to legalize and control the terror that was everywhere breaking out spontaneously. Hostages, counterrevolutionists, officers, well-known members of the bourgeoisie were executed by the hundreds. The Russian Revolution had its September days, its

Fouquier-Tinvilles, its Carriers, its Jean-Lebons, its Fouches —
and the Fouches in particular had a radiant future ahead of
them. The same historic situation in two different countries
and at intervals of a hundred and twenty-five years produced
the same effects with the same result, which was to raise all
the energies of the revolution to the highest pitch in a situation
that was almost desperate.

The first Red troops retreat on every occasion. Kazan, the
key to the Volga, is lost. Trotsky, Ivan Smirnov, and a group
of militants arrive by special train in the midst of this debacle.
They themselves — followed only by the personnel of the train —
join battle in Svyazhsk — and gain a decisive victory. The
next day Trotsky enters the port of Kazan on board a gun-
boat and sets fire to the White fleet.

Our luck had changed. The morale of the troops recovered.
Trotsky signed this order:

> The soldiers of the workers' and peasants' Red Army are
> not cowardly rabble. They want to fight for the liberty and
> happiness of the working people. If they retreat or fight
> badly, it is the fault of the commanders and commissars.
>
> I serve notice that if a unit gives ground, the political
> commissar will first be shot. Then the commander.
>
> Courageous soldiers will be rewarded in accordance with
> their merits. They will receive commands.
>
> The cowards, the traitors, and profiteers will not escape
> our bullets. For this I assume responsibility before the Red
> Army.

Many revolutionists disapproved this manner of speech and
action, but Lenin approved it heartily. In any case, the defeat
was ended. Kazan was retaken; the Red Army was reconsti-
tuted out of nothing, became day by day stronger and began
to be victorious almost everywhere, despite the technical intervention of the Western powers in favor of the Whites.

Through the civil war that they have begun, the former propertied classes lose everything. The logic of the struggle demands
this. The famine necessitates rationing in the cities and requisitions in the country where, as a result, peasant uprisings break
out. To an ever increasing extent, the economy must be directed
with a view to war, and stringent measures of nationalization
are extended to the whole of production. Factory owners ask
to be nationalized, as they cannot live otherwise. In the fall of
1919, the Whites under Admiral Kolchak are the masters of
Siberia; they constitute the "supreme government" of the Ukraine

under General Denikin, who is preparing for a march on Moscow. In the north, thanks to British battalions, they dominate a vaguely socialist government presided over by old Tchaikowsky, a veteran of the first struggles against czarism; and General Yudenich is preparing to take Petrograd, where the people are dying of hunger in the streets and dead horses are piled up in front of the Grand Opera. All that remains of the soviets is the old Duchy of Muscovy, and that too is menaced. Then in one month a veritable miracle occurs. Yudenich is crushed under the very walls of Petrograd, where Trotsky has set up barricades; a defeat north of Orel disposes of Denikin; his army, harassed in the rear by Makhno and his black* troops, disintegrates and finally, in total disarray, boards ship at Novorossisk; a Red Army, led by Ivan Smirnov, hurls the Whites back in the Urals, while the Red guerrillas begin their pitiless campaigns in Siberia. A few months later Admiral Kolchak is handed over to the Reds by Allied officers afraid for their own skins, and shot one moonlit night near Irkutsk with one of his weeping ministers. Their bodies are thrown into the Angara through a hole dug in the ice.

In 1920 the English set sail from Archangel, 15 as the French set sail from Odessa the year before; 16 a Revolutionary Committee, presided over by Ivan Smirnov, organizes Soviet Siberia. Dzerzhinksy, the head of the Cheka — the extraordinary commission which was the organ of the terror — was just suggesting the abolition of the death penalty when Joseph Pilsudski, the former terrorist of the Polish Socialist Party, decided the moment had come to hurl his troops against Kiev. The Poles entered Kiev just before the Second Congress of the Communist International. But at this moment the Red Army includes almost two million men. The country is looking forward to peace. The national sentiment is so strong that old generals like Polivanov and Brussilov appeal to the former officers to take up arms. Trotsky's train is at all points of the front. The Poles are driven from Kiev. Lenin at once conceives the project of an offensive against Warsaw to make Poland a Soviet state, thereby scrapping the Treaty of Versailles, whose fatal consequences he has just denounced. A Revolutionary Committee for Poland is formed with Marklevsky and Dzerzhinsky at its head; the Sixth Army, led by Tukhachevsky and Smilga, advances on Warsaw in spite of the objections of Trotsky, who considers this immense operation too risky. The workers and peasants of Poland fail to rise, and this once again proves that the revolution cannot

*Refers to the black flag of the anarchists. — V. S.

be brought into a foreign country at the point of a gun. Pilsudski, supported by Weygand, wins the battle of Warsaw. Russia loses a common border with Germany, and Germany loses its chance of revolution.

These immense efforts have raised the tension in the interior to the highest pitch. The entire system rests on the discipline of the party, on organized famine in the cities, on requisitions in the country. The consequence is peasant uprisings, at the end of 1920 and the beginning of 1921. The most serious of these is in the region of Tambov, where the peasant army attains a force of 80,000 men under the leadership of a former schoolteacher by the name of Antonov. In the Ukraine, Makhno attempts to form an anarchist federation in the region of Gulai-Polye. An opposition grows within the party, dissatisfied with its authoritarian centralism. The Kronstadt sailors rebel.

I followed these events very closely, and it seems to me unquestionable that measures taken in time could easily have countered all these evils. It would have been relatively simple to reach a compromise with Kronstadt and avoid useless massacres in the very heart of the revolution. The danger made the Central Committee merciless, and we must admit that the danger was great. An exhausted Russia was in no condition to resume the revolutionary effort. In the wake of the Kronstadt sailors, we feared uprisings of a totally different sort, a peasant reaction which would have destroyed everything. The Kronstadt situation was settled by cannon brought up over the ice. Then Lenin understood that a change of direction was necessary and put forward the NEP — the New Economic Policy. This meant an end to requisitions, free trade in grain, concessions to foreign capitalists, tolerance toward the small trader, the artisan, and even small-scale industry.

Less than a year later the country was pacified, the famine ended. The old wounds were healing. The future could be viewed with confidence.

THE THIRD INTERNATIONAL

The Communist International was founded in 1919 in Moscow. Two Frenchmen attended its first conference: Henri Guilbeaux and Jacques Sadoul. The former had been condemned to death for communicating with the enemy, while the latter was nearly convicted of the same offense. The German, Eberlein, was sent by the Spartacus League to argue in favor of deferring the foundation of an International, regarded as premature by Rosa Luxemburg and her group. (Rosa had just been assassinated in Berlin along with Karl Liebknecht.) Subkhi, a Turk, who was soon to be massacred by the Kemalists, represented his country. . . .

. . . I am today the sole survivor among the early administrative staff of the CI. I was working in the second district of Petrograd when Zinoviev sent for me; that same evening a group of militiamen whom I had been instructing in certain subjects escorted me through the total darkness of the street, lest I be robbed of the pound of black bread I had with me. In one of the vast, empty rooms of the Smolny Institute, I met a tall, ageless fellow in a shabby soldier's blouse (I happened to be wearing a magnificent Austrian officer's tunic— clothes were becoming scarce). He had a high forehead, spectacles. There was something ascetic, smiling, yet immensely serious about him. He introduced himself:

"Vladimir Mazin (Lichtenstadt), old Maximalist, ten years in Schluesselburg. And you?"

"Thirteen years of revolutionary activity in three countries, five of imprisonment, nineteen months of internment, etc."

That meant we could work together. Now that we were in power, we were surrounded by revolutionists of the latest vintage, who would have been glad to turn against us at the first sign of bad weather. Already they occupied a good many offices, each one demanding his little bit of power, his special ration of herring and tobacco—and an automobile at the first possibility. Thus, our exchange of references was not useless.

The executive committee of the CI existed only on paper. Zinoviev attended to everything, occasionally consulting Lenin, but more often Radek and Bukharin, who put in brief appearances in our office. Mazin and I were emissaries, functionaries, secretaries, editors, translators, printers, organizers, directors, "members of the collegium," and then some. There were tragicomic moments, such as when Zinoviev summoned me (we lived next door to one another, defended by the same machine gun) and announced in great haste:

"It seems that the English are landing tomorrow. Maybe we're done for, but we're going to try to handle them. You know English. You must write some leaflets and pamphlets at once. . . ."

"But look here, Gregory Yevseich, I don't know enough English. . . ."

"That doesn't matter. Do the best you can. The Cheka has

an Englishman in prison— I've been having plenty of trouble over him — he will help you with the English. . . ."

Mazin was a man of rare moral qualities and unusual intelligence, one of the finest, most complete men I have met in all my life. He was the last survivor of the terrorist group that had blown up Stolypin's villa. The revolution had liberated him from the Schluesselburg where he had shared a cell with Ordjonikidze. In prison he had written a great book on Goethe. Today he is at rest beneath the granite flags of the Leningrad drillground; he was killed defending the city. He said to me: "We have had to take on ourselves the right to decide the life and death of others; we must, therefore, set an example." He set an example.

The first days of the International were the days of heroic camaraderie. We lived in boundless hope. There were rumblings of revolution in the whole of Europe. Manuilsky returned from France— it is true that he understood nothing of what he had seen there — and proved to us that the demobilization marked the beginning of a revolution. He drew this conclusion from a splendid demonstration he had witnessed. Ridel, returning from Italy (he is dead, so I can name him), was less optimistic: in Italy the revolution was in men's hearts and in the nature of things, but had found no leaders. Only one man dared to affirm its possibility: the anarchist Malatesta. The socialists feared it. Mussolini and his gangs had offered their services; should they be accepted? Shablin, later murdered in Bulgaria, said with fine assurance: "We shall take power when we so desire." Soviets came to power in Munich and Budapest. In Vienna, Doctor Bettelheim embarked on an adventure which was quickly disowned.

And the dead mingled with the living. Levine was quickly executed in Munich; Tibor Szamuely, who had spoken to us but a short time before in Moscow, blew out his brains, escaping from the defeat of Red Hungary (in reality more swindled than defeated by old Clemenceau, who had persuaded Bela Kun to halt a victorious offensive). . . . Corvin was hanged in Budapest. Muna arrived from Czechoslovakia, reporting that the lid was about to blow off there. Bela Kun coming from Vienna was (in a single session) twenty times called an imbecile by Lenin for an inept attempt at a putsch in Berlin. He subsequently went to the Crimea where he organized the most atrocious and useless massacres of our revolution. Rakhia, the Finn, who was shortly to be shot by his own party comrades, came and went discreetly from one frontier to another. The American, John Reed, athletic and good-humored, was released from prison in Finland. He died in 1921.

Then with victory came the great flourishing — I was going to say "vogue" — of the International. So many people joined it, now that they felt it was becoming a power, that the Russians decided to take precautions against politicians, opportunists, and adventurers: these precautions were the twenty-one conditions for membership which split the unified Socialist Party of France at Tours, the Independent Social Democratic Party of Germany at Halle, the Italian Socialist Party at Livorno. Mingled with the revolutionists, politicians put in an appearance at the Kremlin: Marcel Cachin, yesterday's arch-patriot (and still a patriot at heart), suddenly converted to militant internationalism. L.-O. Frossard came with him, looking very wise. The brilliant Bordiga denounced Lenin's opportunism at every opportunity, and in the evening led parades of singing students through the delegates' hotel; the Hindu, Manabendra Nath Roy, came in search of arguments and munitions for agitation in India, and apparently found happiness in the arms of a Mexican girl as slender and beautiful as he, but dazzlingly blonde. The Hungarian, Rudniansky, was to turn traitor (he is now in the Solovietski Islands, I have been assured). Among the Italians, there were old Lazzari, Serrati, Angelica Balabanoff, representing the tradition of Italian socialism; young Terracini of the *Ordine Nuovo;* among the English: Sylvia Pankhurst, Gallacher, later Newbold; the Dutch: Wijnkoop, Sneevliet; among the French: Raymond Lefevre, poet and thinker, meditating on *Revolution or Death;* the anarchist, Lepetit, a sturdy young fellow; Vergeat, of the Metal Workers; Rosmer, silent and hard-working, in whom one immediately sensed an absolute probity and devotion; Fernand Loriot, forty-eight years old, but a revolutionist of the war days; Boris Souvarine, biting, imperious, unruly, perpetually asking embarrassing questions. Among the Germans: Paul Levi, who had the appearance of a young Marxist statesman. Angel Pestana brought us the adherence of the Spanish CNT. Some time later a young Catalan teacher with severe features arrived in Moscow: he was Joaquin Maurin. And with him, a laughing young fellow with gold-rimmed spectacles: Andres Nin; Vuyo Vuyovich, bold and crafty, who at twenty-five was an old "professional revolutionist," gaily crossed all the frontiers of Europe.

The Russians at the Congress were: Lenin, with his astounding simplicity; Trotsky, erect in a white tunic, attending between journeys; Karl Radek, malicious, voluble, monkey-like, the most satanic of debaters; Zinoviev, the inexhaustible chairman, with his long, unruly hair; Bukharin, in whom science became amusing and almost juvenile.

The Third International of the early days, for which men fought and many died, which filled the prisons with martyrs, was in reality a great moral and political force, not only because following the war the workers' revolution was on the ascendant in Europe and was very nearly victorious in several countries, but because it brought together a multitude of passionate, sincere, devoted minds determined to live and die for communism. The mountebanks and petty adventurers hardly counted in the ensemble. Where are all these men today?

Lazzari, Serrati, Loriot are dead. Paul Levi, expelled from the Party, committed suicide during an attack of delirium. Lefevre, Lepetit, Vergeat are dead.* Terracini has been in prison in Italy for many years. Roy, expelled from the Party, is in prison in India. [17] Balabanoff, expelled, is an active socialist. Bordiga, expelled, enjoys a strictly limited liberty in Italy. Faithful to their convictions, Rosmer, Souvarine (and with them Pierre Monatte and Jacques Mesnil, French communists of the earliest days), were expelled long ago. Vuyo Vuyovich is in prison in Russia at Verkhne-Uralsk. All the Russians for that matter. . . . Joaquin Maurin, founder of the POUM in Spain, expelled and slandered by the official CP, was shot by the Spanish fascists; [18] expelled and banished from the USSR, Andres Nin, Minister of Justice in the Catalonian Generalidad,† is denounced daily by the local Stalinist press as an "agent of international fascism" (sic); [19] Sylvia Pankhurst and Newbold have been expelled; gone also is the indefatigable Sneevliet. . . .[20]

The CI has squandered its forces, disdained its great talents, dispersed, hunted, persecuted the men of good will who came from the ends of the earth to offer their services. . . .

THE NEP AND THE OPPOSITION

In a few years time the NEP restored to Russia an aspect of prosperity. But to many of us this prosperity was some-

---

*Permit me once again to refute here the odious legend surrounding their deaths at sea. I was well acquainted with the circumstances of their departure. I was the companion of their last days in Russia, and I know that their deaths resulted solely from an accident facilitated by their own impatience. — V. S.

†Nin was removed from this post, following the expulsion of the POUM from the Generalidad. — V. S.

times distasteful and often disquieting. The socialist power retained all the levers of government and maneuvered them ably with its personnel of revolutionary workers and intellectuals. At least seven-eighths of industrial production was nationalized. The nation breathed once more: life began to be more pleasant; breaths of liberalism touched the ruling circles. Writers encountered a tolerance such as today seems unheard of, a tolerance which made possible several real masterpieces. Kamenev, chairman of the Moscow Soviet and of the Supreme Council of Labor and Defense, spoke of authorizing the publication of a daily paper independent of the party. . . . The general level of wages somewhat exceeded the prewar scale; consumption was slightly below the prewar level.

A persistent anxiety took hold of us communists. We had accepted all the necessities of the revolution, including the hardest and most repulsive; we had seen the best among us go to their death; we had submitted to the bitterest constraint in expectation of the harvest. Then, immediately following the Kronstadt killings — our blackest memory — Lenin gave the signal for retreat, saying: "We must learn from the bourgeoisie. We must learn how to carry on commerce; we shall sell everything except alcohol and icons"* -- and almost all of us agreed that he was right, for the previous regime with its requisitions, its total nationalization of distribution (born of the war and not of any preconceived intention), was obviously untenable. And now the cities we ruled over assumed a foreign aspect; we felt ourselves sinking into the mire — paralyzed, corrupted. . . . Money lubricated and befouled the entire machine just as under capitalism. A million and a half unemployed received relief — inadequate relief — in the big towns. Saloons were open until three o'clock in the morning in the heart of the cities. There was gambling, drunkenness, and all the old filth of former times. We knew that most of the money thus squandered had been stolen from us; we knew the state had been cheated out of this money by crooked brokers and functionaries. The bathing establishments and hotels were haunted by painted women, resembling in every way their sisters of Whitechapel or Barbes. Classes were reborn under our very eyes; at the bottom of the scale, the unemployed receiving 24 rubles a month; at the top, the engineer receiving 800; and between the two, the party functionary with 222,

---

*In this he was mistaken. Not long after his death the Politbureau decided, against the votes of Krupskaya, his widow, and of Trotsky, to restore the alcohol monopoly, suppressed by Nicholas II at the beginning of the war. The sale of vodka adds precious revenue to the budget of the USSR but costs the people dear. — V. S.

but obtaining a good many things free of charge. There was a growing chasm between the prosperity of the few and the misery of the many; there were countless suicides. There was talk of broadening the rights of inheritance. Stalin proposed in a barely veiled form the restoration of landed property for the rich peasants. There was squalid, heartbreaking poverty, an ulcer in our young society, while wealth was arrogant and self-satisfied. Our socialist militia arrested the poor apple-woman who neglected to take out a license, while the fat shopkeeper, enriched by the sale at speculative prices of articles manufactured by our socialist industry, looked on and decided that by and large, order was returning. . . . The young people drank, old people drank, drunkenness became a plague. And worst was that we could no longer recognize the old party of the revolution. The old militants, those who had experience of prison and the love of ideas, were only a handful; and these few were placed in jobs isolating them from the rank and file. Even those who had joined during the civil war felt lost in the wave of late comers, the comfortable new conformists who at bottom cared exceedingly little about the future of the proletarian revolution, desiring only to live in comfort and without complications. Shortsighted and unintelligent, like all petty profiteers, they did not understand that such tactics lead to more and worse complications later on.

Our anxiety at seeing this degradation of the state and these first symptoms of the bourgeoisification of Soviet society was, of course, not emotional; it was intellectual and based on economic data. Lenin died — on January 21, 1924 — haunted by this anxiety, which is expressed in his last writings and speeches. "Is not the helm escaping from our hands?" he asked. Ill, stricken in his brain, he had spent his last strength in seeking arms against the worst and most immediate evil: the bureaucratic degeneration of the party. Already bureaus were replacing the party; the worker, the militant rank-and-filer hardly dared open his mouth. We sensed the coming omnipotence of the functionaries. Some few announced that the dictatorship of the proletariat was being replaced by the dictatorship of the secretariat (the epigram is Souvarine's). Shortly before his death, Lenin proposed to Trotsky — who was hostile to the bureaucratic system — an action in common for the democratization of the party. As General Secretary, the Georgian, Stalin, obscure during the civil war, was becoming more and more influential, using his technical functions to fill the various bureaus with his creatures. He was the obstacle to Lenin's last efforts, and the last letter dictated by Vladimir

Ilyich when the finger of death was upon him, was a letter of rupture addressed to Stalin.

In terms of economic policy, the problem was expressed by the relationship between industry and agriculture. The latter was recovering more rapidly than industry; the peasant accumulated reserves of grain because he was offered too low a price for it; and the low price of wheat resulted in high prices for manufactured goods, whose quantity was not up to the demand. The country was approaching an irremediable economic crisis, a crisis which might arouse a hundred and twenty million peasants against the socialist power and place it at the mercy of foreign capital by forcing it to import (on credit? and under what conditions?) great quantities of manufactured goods. To forestall this crisis certain measures had to be taken before it was too late.

These measures were:

1. To restore democracy in the party, so that the influence of the workers might be felt; to ventilate the state bureaus. This was the obvious condition for the success of all economic measures.

2. To adopt a plan for industrialization and appreciably rebuild industry within a few years.

3. In order to obtain the resources necessary for industrialization, force the well-to-do peasants to deliver their wheat to the state.

In general to limit the private acquisition of wealth and privilege, to combat speculation, to limit the power of the functionaries.

This was the gist of the program of the Opposition in the party. Hence its slogan: "Against the merchant, the rich peasant, and the bureaucrat."

Beginning in 1923, the Opposition found a leader in Trotsky; the bureaucratic system began to find its incarnation in Stalin.

Beginning in 1923, an agitational campaign unlimited in its violence was launched against Trotsky; he was everywhere denounced as anti-Leninist, the evil spirit of the party, the enemy of the Bolshevik tradition, the enemy of the peasants. His old disagreements with Lenin, dating from 1904 to 1915, were exploited by professional polemicists under Stalin's orders; under the name of Trotskyism they forged an entire, distorted ideology which was made into the most criminal heresy. In vain Trotsky's brilliant pen uttered the most consistent thoughts. The official press, circulated in the millions, smothered his voice, and tirelessly hammered away at its campaign of falsification. We subsequently learned the inside story of these cam-

paigns; we learned that neither error nor passion was behind
this deliberate falsification of facts and ideas. We have a number
of signed statements, regarding the "fabrication" of Trotskyism . . . (though it is true that several of their authors
were recently shot).

At first, the organizer of the Red Army, still chairman of the
Supreme War Council and acclaimed by *Pravda* but a few
months before as the "organizer of the victory," was so popular
in the army and throughout the country that he might, with
good chances of success, have attempted a coup. But in so
doing, he would simply have had to substitute army rule for
bureau rule; such a coup would have started the socialist revolution on the track hitherto pursued by bourgeois revolutions.
And his aim was not to play the Bonaparte, even with the
best of intentions, but, on the contrary, to prevent bonapartism.
It was not by a pronunciamento that the Opposition sought
to bring about the inner renewal of the revolution, but by the
time-honored socialist method of appealing to the workers.
Trotsky relinquished his executive positions, let himself be demoted without resistance, resumed his place in the rank and
file—and the struggle continued. Everything, in the last analysis, depends on the international situation. After the failure of
the revolution in Germany in 1923 (the Chemnitz Conference,
the Hamburg insurrection, the violent repression of the workers'
government of Saxony, the dictatorship of General von Seeckt,)
a wave of depression passed over Russia, and the bureaucracy
had its own way for three years.

ZINOVIEV

During this period Gregory Zinoviev was the leading member
of the Politbureau; Kamenev the second; and Stalin the third.
"Lenin's co-worker since 1907, theoretician, popularizer and
orator—an unruly shock of hair, a somewhat flabby, clean-
shaven face, a careless appearance, well-rounded gestures, a
low voice which can become strident when he wants to be
sure of being heard, a ruthless tongue"—Zinoviev is the chairman of the Soviet in Petrograd, which he renames Leningrad
by decree, and has been the chairman of the Communist International since its foundation. His drama, which now com-
mences, proceeds from a profound conviction, a certain ambition, and a distinct mediocrity of character.

His capacities as an agitator cut him out to be the indefatigable second of someone greater than himself in thought
and character. In twenty years of day-to-day work he made

himself the mouthpiece, the factotum, the popularizer of Lenin. Now that Vladimir Ilyich was dead, he considered himself destined to succeed him. In the International he was a man of shady little schemes; at home, the exponent of repression. Into ideological struggles, he introduces intrigue and trickery in increasing doses; by gradual steps he introduces repression in the party: nonetheless the defeats of the CI, of whose incompetent leadership there can be no doubt, rebound to his discredit. From 1923 to 1925, he joined forces with Stalin to keep Trotsky from the power to which his unlimited popularity and Lenin's known choice entitled him. People began to whisper that Lenin had left a sort of testament, which had been concealed by the Central Committee. It was not long before this text passed from hand to hand. In it Lenin gave evidence of a perspicacity which history has only too well confirmed. All his judgements on his co-workers have since been verified. ". . . The October episode of Zinoviev and Kamenev was not, of course, accidental . . ." he says. Bukharin is a remarkable theoretician, but somewhat prone to scholasticism.

> . . . Comrade Trotsky . . . is distinguished not only by his exceptional ability — personally, he is, to be sure, the most able man in the present Central Committee — but also by his too far-reaching self-confidence and a disposition to be far too much attracted by the purely administrative side of affairs.
>
> These two qualities of the two most able leaders of the present Central Committee might, quite innocently, lead to a split. . . .
>
> Stalin is too rude, and this fault, entirely supportable in relations among us communists, becomes unsupportable in the office of General Secretary. Therefore, I propose to the comrades to find a way to remove Stalin from that position and appoint another man who in all respects differs from Stalin only in superiority — namely, more patient, more loyal, more polite and more attentive to comrades, less capricious, etc. This circumstance may seem an insignificant trifle, but I think that from the point of view of the relation between Stalin and Trotsky which I discussed above, it is not a trifle, or it is such a trifle as may acquire a decisive significance.[21]

Lenin wrote these lines on January 4, 1923, less than a year before his death. In other confidential notes he castigates the brutality of Ordjonikidze and pronounces a severe

judgment on the Soviet state. It is "a bourgeois czarist machine . . . barely varnished with socialism." He commends
Piatakov as one of the good administrators, with important
reservations as to his political abilities. . . .

From this time on, Stalin demonstrated a consummate ability at intrigue and the manipulation of the party controls.
At the outset, the fight against Trotskyism astounded the country. The revolution, accustomed in the main to rough, healthy
ways, did not expect this deluge of lies, of veiled slanders,
of manufactured revelations — this heartbreaking schism of its
leaders who until then had seemed to be admirably united.
The party did not expect this sudden intrusion of the mailed
fist into its inner life.

Stalin intimates that he played the part of peacemaker; that
he was opposed to expulsions; opposed to "the letting of
blood" — thus permitting all the unpopularity of his campaigns
to fall on Zinoviev. He likewise maneuvers so as to make
Zinoviev and Kamenev appear responsible for all the failures
of the agrarian policy which led to the enrichment of a minority of peasants and a critical shortage in the state grain
collections. He lets Zinoviev take the responsibility for the
defeats of the International. In the corridors of the Kremlin
he is overheard saying that the branches of the CI are full
of "clowns, bluffers, and paid politicians," and that if he were
the master, he would promptly "cut off their credit, for those
people can no longer be of any service to the cause of the
revolution. . . ."

In the meantime Stalin completes the job of packing all the
party secretariats (excepting those of the Leningrad region,
controlled by Zinoviev) with his creatures. In 1926 his work
is done; he is the master of the party, of a party in whose
ranks utter silence reigns, a party in which majorities, docile
because they profit by being docile, do nothing but vote the
resolutions prescribed by the Central Committee and submitted
by the secretaries. At the Fourteenth Congress, Zinoviev is
suddenly put in the minority, isolated, and rendered responsible
for all internal and foreign difficulties. . . . It is not too late
for him to retire to a secondary position, as several others
do, and retain his small share of power. But despite everything the socialist in him is stronger and more devoted than
the statesman, even stronger than ambition. The controversy
turns on questions of prime importance. Stalin announces the
new policy of "socialism in one country," which would be totally meaningless if it did not signify a renunciation of international solidarity. No compromise is possible. Stalin enters

into combination with the rightists of the CC (Rykov, Tomsky, Bukharin) to continue an agrarian policy of enriching the kulaks. Stalin completes his task of strangling the party: Zinoviev goes over to the Opposition; in an embarrassing about-face his joins his adversary of the day before, Trotsky, accepting his program for democratization of the party—and consequently of the government—for industrialization and pressure on the "kulak, the nepman, and the bureaucrat." The Chinese Revolution tragically sharpens the struggle.

THE COMMUNIST INTERNATIONAL AND
THE CHINESE REVOLUTION

There had been six large parties in the Third International: those of France, Germany, Italy, Bulgaria, Yugoslavia, and Czechslovakia. Since the defeat of the proletarian revolution in Finland, Hungary, Germany, and Italy (1918-1922), the International had been able to raise the question of power in Germany and in Bulgaria; but these attempts had led to disaster, without bloodshed in Germany,[22] with dreadful massacres in Bulgaria.[23] The cause of the proletarian revolution in the West seemed lost for many years to come. And now an immense light was rising in the East; the Chinese masses had been stirred from their apathy, and were advancing from victory to victory. Hong Kong was blockaded by Canton, a revolutionary republic was formed in south China, with Soviet advisers and instructors, Borodin in the Cabinet, Galen (that is, Bluecher, the former guerrilla chief of the Urals) in Chiang Kai-shek's new-formed army, Voitinsky in Peking. Lenin was growing as popular as Sun Yat-sen. Galen-Bluecher led Chiang Kai-shek's army northward, the trade unions took possession of Shanghai and Hankow. Everyone wondered what revolutionary power would arise out of the victory of a workers' and peasants' revolution throughout the extent of the yellow continent. The destinies of Eurasia were changing, and with them the destiny of our times. Yet we knew the inside of these victories; with our own eyes we saw the workers of Shanghai, Canton, Hankow, and Nanking led into ambush by our bureaucrats.

By this time the bureaucracy has, in actual fact, driven the workers from power in the USSR. Of the dictatorship of the proletariat, only the name remains. In the key positions, revo-

lutionists have been replaced by functionaries. Policies are
no longer inspired by the general interests of the Russian and
international proletariat, but by the functionaries' wish not to
be bothered. Stalin becomes their idol. They fear the victory
of the Chinese Revolution even more than they pretend to desire it. They never dare when the hour for daring has struck.
Their entire tactics consist in maneuvers to avoid complications.
This leads to worse complications, but then it is too late.

We *know* that Chiang Kai-shek is preparing the open betrayal of the unions and his communist allies. We know that
he is preparing a coup against the proletariat of Shanghai,
which has accomplished one of the finest insurrections in modern history. We are not permitted to speak. And Stalin takes
the floor in Moscow before thousands of workers and solemnly
assures them that we have nothing to fear from Chiang Kai-
shek. "We shall break him after having made use of him."
This speech had not yet been published when, on the following
day, the wires informed us of the event we had predicted: the
massacre of the workers of Shanghai (1927). Stalin has the
text and the proofs of his unfortunate speech removed from
the office of *Pravda;* they will never be seen again. He is reduced to stealing his own speech.*

On all this I shall quote only one document of the time, the
report delivered at the Fifteenth Party Congress by Chitarov,
a Russian communist who had been sent to China. Stalin uses
it to condemn those who, in China, had faithfully executed his
orders. . . .

> For twenty days there was in Shanghai a people's gov-
> ernment in which the communists had the majority. . . .
> This government was inactive although a military coup
> was expected at any moment . . . because the government
> of Wuhan had not confirmed it in its power (this govern-
> ment included two communist ministers). . . . Hsueh Yoh,
> the leader of the first division, came to the comrades and in-
> formed them of the preparations for the coup . . . he was
> ready to join us with his troops against the military. The
> leaders of the CP replied that they knew about the plot
> but did not wish to break with Chiang Kai-shek premature-
> ly; they ordered Hsueh Yoh to go to the front or to resign
> by way of proving his loyalty to the general. The first
> division left the city; the second replaced it; and two days

---

*Malraux in **Man's Fate** has thrown some light on these episodes.
His previous book, **The Conquerors,** was banned in the USSR. **Man's
Fate** has not yet been translated into Russian, and if it does appear
in Russian, it will not be without the characteristic mutilations. — V. S.

later the workers of Shanghai were shot down en masse.

The Kremlin's policies were bearing splendid fruit. And this was only the beginning.

> During the period when the revolutionary forces have reached their highest pitch, the Chinese CP [read: the Communist International] beats an unceasing, systematic retreat. It consents to submit all its organizations, trade unions, peasant leagues, etc. to the Kuomintang; it renounces all initiative without authorization of the Kuomintang; it orders the voluntary disarmament of the workers of Hankow; consents de facto to the violent liquidation of all the peasants' organizations. . . .
> . . . in Hunan the counterrevolution triumphed on the twenty-first and twenty-second of May (1927) under circumstances which are hardly credible. There were 1700 troops in the capital and 20,000 organized and armed peasants in the environs. However, the officers succeeded in taking power, in shooting the peasant leaders and establishing their dictatorship. . . . The peasants were on the point of taking possession of the city, which they could have done without difficulty, when they received a message from the Central Committee of the CP ordering them to avoid an armed conflict and to pose the question through governmental channels. The provincial committee sent the Red detachments the order to retreat. Two detachments did not receive the order on time; they attacked, and were surrounded and exterminated . . . [24]

Today, beneath my pen these are little black lines like other lines, but how much poor men's blood they represent no one will ever know. May they serve to enlighten other workers in a country nearer to us, constrained by force of circumstances to accept and submit to the authoritarian counsel of those responsible for what happened then.

What is the blood of Chinese workers to Stalin? Facing the Fifteenth Congress, he must attempt to counterbalance the effect of all these defeats and of the mass expulsions he has just pronounced (for, previous to the Congress, no longer daring to face debate on his responsibilities, he has had his principal adversaries, Trotsky and Zinoviev, expelled for infraction of discipline). He requires a victory in China, if only for an hour; and if he cannot have a victory, a few more thousand heroic martyrs. In this case all criticism could be stifled by

invoking the respect for the dead and "in order not to play
into the hands of reaction." He sends to Canton his cousin
Lominadze and Heinz Neumann, a young German as courageous as he was unscrupulous, to embark on a new revolutionary effort. . . .

    . . . So on the night of December 10, by a coincidence
with the Congress, leaving no doubt as to its spontaneity,
a local uprising breaks out in Canton. Stalin's agents
have fomented this action in order to obtain for their
chief a victory bulletin as an argument against the "pessi-
mism of the Opposition." The result is a revolutionary
rearguard action, isolated, artificial, and doomed to failure.
The Canton Commune, surrounded by the military forces
of the Kuomintang, lasted only forty-eight hours; its fall
was accompanied by a dreadful slaughter. More than 2000*
communists, or supposed communists, are massacred or
tortured on the spot. At the Congress, one of Stalin's emissaries in China reported that about 30,000 Chinese workers
had been put to death; in a period of only five months
from April to August 1927, after the mad Canton putsch
and the bloody repression which prolonged its echo for
several weeks, the most conservative observers estimate
a total of about 100,000 vicitims of the incoherent policies
pursued under the aegis of "Moscow." Chinese communism
is just about annihilated. A handful of survivors, among
them the former secretary, Chen Tu-hsiu, went over to the
Opposition and were expelled from the party.† Thus ends
the cycle of aberrations and adventures from which Stalin,
at the price of 100,000 human lives, emerges forever dis-
qualified as a theoretician and strategist of the revolution. [25]

This is the historian's point of view. In reality, Stalin emerges
from these unspeakable disasters fortified and almost glorified.
The defeat of the revolution in Asia assures his victory at home.
In Russia, the revolutionary spirit is gravely compromised.
More than ever "socialism in one country" is valid, because
the revolution has been defeated everywhere else. Enough complications. The epigones wish to take it easy, to have done
with adventures. . . . What a fist he has, this Georgian! Long
live the fist! ‡

---

    *Actually 5700 were killed. — Translator.

    †A number of them were imprisoned in the Soviet Union. The
son of Chen Tu-hsiu was beheaded in Shanghai. — V. S.

    ‡Not so long ago, in 1934-1935 and even in the first months

The subalterns were not to be so kindly treated by fate. Lominadze, his cousin, who turned Oppositionist after these events, blew out his brains in Sverdlovsk in 1935 when about to be arrested. Heinz Neumann has disappeared from the scene; he is said to be imprisoned in the Soviet Union. He had permitted himself some critical remarks; and he knows too much. Several of the young unknowns, shot with Zinoviev, were his political associates.

From Paris, Berlin, London, Guatemala; from everywhere, the Central Committees of the Communist parties, appointed and paid by him, wire their approval of everything: the friendship of Chiang Kai-shek, the expulsions, Canton, the eternal correctness of the policies of the Executive of the CI, the whole absurd, bloody business. Thaelmann — who never wearies of announcing the inevitable seizure of power in Germany — Doriot, Barbusse, Marcel Cachin, and all the others approve, greet with enthusiasm, approve everything — *everything*.

DISCORD IN THE CENTRAL COMMITTEE

The last meetings of the Central Committee prior to the expulsion of the leaders of the Opposition (end of October 1927) were tempestuous. They are reminiscent of the session of the Convention in which Robespierre could not make himself heard. Let us excerpt a few characteristic passages from the *official* minutes, in which obviously the insults have been attenuated.

> *Trotsky:* Through the present apparatus, through the present regime, the proletarian vanguard undergoes the pressure . . . [*The noise increases more and more. The orator can hardly be heard.*] of the upstart bureaucrats including the worker-bureaucrats [Tumult, whistling], of the administrators, the petty bosses, the new-born proprietors, the privileged intellectuals of city and country. . . .
>
> *Voroshilov:* Zinoviev, it's outrageous!

of 1936, the Soviet press and the Communist press throughout the world made much to-do over the victories of the soviets in China. What has become of these soviets? Or rather, what has been done to them? — V. S.

Skrypnik: The platform of the Central Committee wasn't made for such infamy.*

Skvortsov-Stepanov: He's Dan, the Menshevik, in disguise.

Trotsky: The pressure of all those elements who are beginning to show the proletariat their fists, saying: "It is no longer 1918." It is not the leftward zigzags which are decisive but our policy as a whole. It is the choice of cadres, the support of the masses. It is impossible to resist the enriched peasants while stifling the proletarian units. These things are incompatible. . . . [*Increasing noise, whistling.*]

Voices: Gravedigger of the revolution! Shame! Down with him! Down with the rascal! The renegade!

Trotsky: Leftward zigzags will encounter the resistance of the majority. Today, "enrich yourselves," but tomorrow [*Noise, cat-calls*] . . . we shall obtain nothing from the rich peasants. . . . Behind the bureaucrats the bourgeoisie is coming back to life. . . . [*Noise, cat-calls, cries of:* "Down with him."]

Voroshilov: That's enough. For shame! [*Whistling, hoots, increasing tumult. Nothing can be heard. The chairman rings his bell; whistling. Voices cry:* "Down from the platform." *The chairman adjourns the meeting. Comrade Trotsky continues to read, but not a word can be distinguished. The members of the Central Committee leave their places and begin to disperse*]26

Zinoviev's speech gets the same reception.

Zinoviev: The lessons of the last years are clear to everyone. We propose only a return to the regime of Lenin.

Voices: Don't confuse it with yours.

Zinoviev: No one demands ideal, perfect democracy. We understand that the times are hard. . . .

Voices: Down with him! Down! [*The chairman rings his bell.*]

Zinoviev: One moment more. [*Noise. The chairman's bell.*]

Voices: Down with him. Get out.

Zinoviev: In two words, our entire fight in the party today revolves around this dilemma: either you will give

---

*Skrypnik, a conspicuous militant since the beginning of the revolution, faithful to Stalin from the outset, committed suicide in 1933 in the Ukraine in the course of a vast campaign of repression against his Ukrainian comrades. — V. S.

us an opportunity to appeal to the party and speak to the party, or you will have to put us in prison. . . . There is no other alternative. . . . [*Laughter, hoots, the chairman rings his bell.*]

Voices: Enough. Down from the platform. Get out. [*Zinoviev descends from the platform amid hoots and cries. Increasing tumult.*]

Almost ten years later (I digress here to show how far the falsification of the past can go under a totalitarian regime) at the Novosibirsk trial on November 21, 1936, the witness Shubin states:

The alliance between the Trotskyists and the accused Stickling, today an agent of the Gestapo, was concluded in 1927. The purpose was to restore capitalism in the USSR and to set up a fascist dictatorship. This decision was taken in a secret conference presided over by Trotsky, which took place in a forest near Moscow.

The court in pronouncing sentence considered these facts as proved, and they were sufficient to justify nine death sentences, one of which affected a German. Six unfortunates were executed after having thus confessed — everything they were instructed to confess.

These scenes in the Central Committee were duplicated in the lower organizations and even in the street. I had occasion to speak, or rather to try to speak, before gatherings shaken with a sort of frenzy. We were given the floor for five minutes after three-hour harangues. And against each one of us they unleashed five, six, sometimes ten "activists" eager to procure the favor of the secretaries. The crowd looked on passively, with a certain anxiety; they were often on our side, but they were afraid. "You understand," said the printers in my unit. "First, there's unemployment in the trade. Besides, I have children. If I join up with you and you are defeated, what's going to become of me and all my kids?" On the anniversary of the October Revolution, we tried to demonstrate, within the ranks of the party, but with our own slogans. I was almost cut to pieces in Leningrad when three hundred of us Oppositionists (among us Lashevich, a former army commander, and Bakayev, a former head of the Cheka) clashed with the militia before the doors of the Hermitage. At Moscow, Smilga, he too an old army chief and one of the founders of the republic, had placed portraits of Lenin and Trotsky on his balcony.

In consequence his house was entered and pillaged. Trotsky was fired on in the street. Two of our people who attempted to set up a sign on the Red Square were beaten unmercifully. Party committees organized strong-arm gangs against us, equipped with whistles and authorized to strike hard; they were transported in trucks to reinforce the right-thinking elements in the meetings where we attempted to speak. In Moscow these fascist proceedings were organized by the secretary of the regional committee, Riutin, a man who happened to be sincere in his blindness. . . .

In 1932, enlightened by the course of events, this Riutin went over to the Opposition. He drew up a draft program in which he called Stalin "the great provocateur, the destroyer of the party." The GPU dubbed his words incitement to assassination and condemned him to death. They did not, however, dare to execute him. No one knows what has become of him.

DEFEATS, PROSCRIPTIONS, CAPITULATIONS

We were beaten, and our defeat did not disturb the general indifference. Was this Thermidor? Or was it not? There was no end of discussions on this theme of historic parallels; and history pursued its course.

The Third International had changed its face. A curious combination of circumstances now brought together in its leadership a number of men, all of whom bore responsibility for its heaviest defeats: docile and comfortable, they had regained favor by passive obedience. Several of them are to this day in the high leadership of the CI where they continue to take it easy. The most conspicuous of them are: Bela Kun, the man of the defeat in Hungary and of some affairs that are even worse from the moral point of view;[27] Kuusinen, who in 1918 contributed mightily to the downfall of proletarian Finland and who subsequently had the merit of admitting it in a highly interesting political confession;[28] Kolarov[29] and Dimitrov,[30] who had three times led the Bulgarian party into unspeakable disasters; and until recently, Heinz Neumann, who reached maturity in the German defeats and showed his full abilities in the Canton catastrophe. . . .

The aspect of the government and the press underwent the same change. In Georgia, Mensheviks had come into power and persecuted old Bolsheviks. While the men who had fought

in 1917 were expelled from the party—soon to be deported—
newcomers, who had been counterrevolutionists during the civil
war, carved out splendid careers for themselves by their zeal
in approving the new leader. Zaslavsky, who had been one
of those to call Lenin a "German agent," occupied a position
of authority on *Pravda*; Vishinsky, a right-wing socialist, who
in 1918 had been involved in the sabotage of the food administration in the Ukraine, became prosecuting attorney at the
supreme court; Maisky, a former member of the counterrevolutionary government of Samara, went into the diplomatic service
(he now represents the USSR in London); another former
enemy, Khinchuk, likewise became a diplomat (he is today
in Berlin). We shall not mention the lesser lights; there are
too many of them. In the party, yesterday's subalterns were
coming to the fore. Men like Kirov, Kuibyshev, Mikoyan—
passable second-raters—or persons entirely unknown during
the great years, such as Kaganovich.

The TASS agency published at the beginning of 1928 a
denial of the "slanderous rumors" to the effect that the Moscow government planned to deport the Oppositionists who
had been expelled from the party. Three or four days after this
denial, the deportations began. Who was deported? The first
group to go included Trotsky; Karl Radek; Preobrazhensky
and Serebriakov, the former secretaries of the Central
Committee; Ivan Smirnov; Beloborodov, one of the real leaders
of the Revolution in the Urals, where he signed the Romanovs'
death sentence; Muralov, Vladimir Smirnov, and Timothy
Sapronov, all three of them heroes of the Moscow insurrection;
Smilga, one of the best heads of the civil war; Rakovsky, who
sustained the revolution in the Ukraine during the hardest
years.

The vocation of defeated revolutionists in a totalitarian state
is a hard one. Many abandon you when they see the game is
lost. Others, whose personal courage and devotion are above
question, think it best to maneuver to adapt themselves to the
circumstances. Piatakov abjures his former convictions and
friendships. In the embassies, Krestinsky, Sokolnikov, Antonov-
Oveenko do likewise. What else can they do? Either they may
take themselves off to the lost villages of Kazakstan or remain,
strive to be of service, and wait. Diplomats—even the diplomats of a revolution—rarely have a stomach for martyr-
dom. . . . They condemn their oppositionist acts and thoughts,
plead for pardon, and debase themselves as much as desired.

Are they opportunists? No. These old Bolsheviks have no
private life outside of their political activity; they attach little

importance to what the bourgeoisie calls position, or even to
happiness. Are they cowards? Ahead of them are nearly ten
years of the most intolerable life, leading up to the most
frightful end. Their attitude combines a great courage, an absolute   devotion   without   phrases   or   gestures — a   courage
which does not hesitate to cloak itself as pusillanimity, a devotion which does not shrink before the worst humiliations — with
a very real intellectual and moral deficiency. Too much attached
to   the   party,   they   fear   to   see   reality   as   it   is.   The
party is finished. They shrink back before this final realization.
They do not sense that in debasing themselves, they debase
the Revolution; that it is better to remain erect and proud in
error than to give an example of such abasement even for
the best of causes. They aim to maneuver, in the belief that the
main thing is to remain within the party until the day when
spontaneously the decisive struggles break out which will make
party reform possible. Radek from his exile castigates their
capitulation. He writes:

> All of Zinoviev's tactical calculations consist in this: a
> new wave must inevitably pass over the party; when this
> happens, we shall be in exile, while he will be in the party.
> But Zinoviev will be deceived in the end. It is the correct-
> ness of one's political views, the confidence one has merited,
> which will be decisive. . . .
>
> The crime of Zinoviev and Kamenev is not to have under-
> stood that we cannot disarm, even if there is a favorable
> turn in the party. . . .

Radek wrote well, but a few months later he did exactly as
Zinoviev and Kamenev had done.

Radek was gifted with an unusual flexibility of mind; out-
wardly he was cynical and witty. He possessed an absolute
devotion to the party, that is, to the working class, whose
political organization is the party. He engaged in revolutionary
activity in Russia, Poland, Austria, and Germany, passed
through many prisons, escaped from innumerable perils; before
becoming Lenin's co-worker, he was the companion in struggle
of Rosa Luxemburg in Berlin, Bremen, and elsewhere. He was
in Berlin with Rosa and Karl Liebknecht when the Spartacist
uprising broke out, which he correctly but vainly advised
against. Arrested together with Karl and Rosa, he was spared
their fate only by chance: his importance was not known. A
bullet grazed him in Moabit prison where his friend Leon
Tyshko (Jogisches) had just been killed.

And now he was once again imprisoned, this time in the USSR. After his capitulation, he meets some Oppositionist comrades firmer than he at a little railroad station in Siberia. They are surrounded by GPU agents conducting them to their respective destinations. We have received the story of this political encounter. It follows:

Radek: The situation of the country is extremely grave. That of the Central Committee is catastrophic. The right and the center are preparing to throw each other into prison. The right is strong. It may double or triple its sixteen votes. Moscow is without bread. . . . The discontent of the working masses may turn against the Soviet system. We are facing peasant uprisings. All this obliges us to return to the party at any cost.

"And what is your attitude toward Lev Davidovich [Trotsky]?"

Radek: Complete rupture. He is revising the doctrine of Lenin.

"Will you demand the abolition of Article 58?" [the article of the penal code under which the Oppositionists were exiled].

Radek: Never. For those who will follow us, it must be upheld. For those who organize discontent among the masses, we shall maintain Article 58. We ourselves were responsible for our deportation and imprisonment. The youth that joins the Opposition has nothing in common with Bolshevism; it is anti-Soviet.

Radek added that the Opposition platform had become that of the party. Proof: the five-year plan. The GPU agents interrupted our discussion. They pushed Radek into the car, reproaching him for agitating against Trotsky's banishment. On the platform of the car, Radek was still crying out:

"I agitate against the banishment of Trotsky? Ha, ha, ha. I was explaining to these comrades that they must return to the party."

And he began to plead with the GPU agents. "Leave them alone. Give them time to reconsider. Don't embitter them."

Without a word the agents pushed him into the car. The express began to move.

Without a word the GPU continued to push Karl Radek for nine years, until they had pushed him into the cell which he now occupies, a few stories above the executioners' cellar. [31]

. . . At the same period, I was expelled from the party to

which I had belonged for eight years. As I could not be re-
proached for infraction of discipline, the Control Commission
asked me if I approved the decision of the Fifteenth Congress
to expel the Opposition. I replied that in this, as in all other
matters, I submitted to party discipline but that I did not approve the decision; I said that I even considered it a costly
error which it would be difficult to repair.

The Commission consisted of ten persons: stupefaction was
visible on all their faces. A working woman arose, doubting
whether she had heard correctly, and asked me in an earnest
voice: "Did you say, comrade, that the party congress was
mistaken? Do you believe that the party congress can be mistaken?"

I explained that to err is human, that great workers' parties
had been known to accumulate mistakes and absurdities and
finally degenerate. With every word I spoke, my heresy increased. I was expelled then and there.

A few days later at about midnight, two young fellows
knocked at my door, one of them in a soldier's cape, the other
in civilian clothes. They seized my correspondence with Barbusse
and a text of Lenin's that aroused their suspicions, and asked
me to follow them. I spent six weeks in a cell in the old Leningrad prison, in company with an engineer of that city, accused
of having sold for his own account a few cubic meters of ice
from the Neva, and a crazy mystic suspected of espionage
because he was a Pole. He was a poor devil, impressively
filthy, who passed his hours kneeling on the cement in prayer;
he had been caught selling crosses near the cemetery and that
had seemed very grave. The little boy who gave us insipid
tea in the morning disappeared one night, shot. One of the
occupants of a nearby cell threw himself from the fifth floor
gallery to the pavement below. This man was a storekeeper,
accused of tax fraud — he must have had weak nerves. Altogether the times were delectable for everybody. My foreign
friends were able to get me out. But afterwards my life was
not an easy one. For to be expelled from the party was to be
a public enemy.

And, of course, everybody understands that neither the books
nor the articles of a public enemy can be published. That his
slightest movements, his correspondence, his words, his re-
lationships will be watched over. That he will not be helped
to earn a living, but will be hindered to some extent. That
he will be paid as little as possible for his work, and that it
will be even better, circumstances permitting, not to pay him
at all. That when, during the famine, the organized writers

share their rations of cheese, honey cake, sausage, and other foodstuffs secretly allotted them by the party committee, either none at all or the least possible will be given to this dangerous nonconformist. You can understand that his wife, his sister-in-law, his brother-in-law, his father-in-law, his cousins and, in case they associate with him, his second cousins, will have all sorts of troubles and very serious ones. Thus, in the course of the years, I assembled a profound knowledge of the workings of a totalitarian state. Until the day when, in the street this time, two citizens with that unmistakable appearance, asked me to follow them. The times were less kindly, and I was not to emerge so soon. But that is another story, of purely secondary interest.

FROM LENIN TO STALIN

Everything has changed.

The aims: from international social revolution to socialism in one country.

The political system: from the workers' democracy of the soviets, the goal of the revolution, to the dictatorship of the general secretariat, the functionaries, and the GPU.

The party: from the organization, free in its life and thought and freely submitting to discipline, of revolutionary Marxists to the hierarchy of bureaus, to the passive obedience of careerists.

The Third International: from a mighty organization of propaganda and struggle to the opportunist servility of Central Committees appointed for the purpose of approving everything, without shame or nausea.

The defeats: from the heroism of the German and Hungarian defeats in which Gustav Landauer, Levine, Liebknecht, Rosa Luxemburg, Jogisches, Otto Corvin met their death, to the heartrending background of the Canton Commune.

The leaders: the greatest militants of October are in exile or prison. From Lenin to Stalin.

The ideology: Lenin said, "We shall see the progressive withering away of the state, and the Soviet state will not be a state like the others, but a vast workers' commune. . . ." Stalin proclaims that "we advance toward the abolition of the state by way of the strengthening of the state" (sic).

The condition of the workers: the equalitarianism of Soviet society is transformed to permit the formation of a privileged minority, more and more privileged in comparison with the disinherited masses who are deprived of all rights.

Morality: from the austere, sometimes implacable honesty of heroic Bolshevism, we gradually advance to unspeakable deviousness and deceit.

Everything has changed, everything is changing, but it will require the perspective of time before we can precisely understand the realities. Too much attachment to the regime, too many illusions about the men, too much love for the land, the country, the dead — too many great memories blind us all, more or less.

It here becomes apparent that moral criteria sometimes have greater value than judgments based on political and economic considerations.

Politics and economics with their infinite complexities permit the deception of statistics and slogans. Even with much knowledge, a clear insight into them is often impossible. While the indignity, the injustice, the traps set for those who only yesterday were comrades, the human degradation, the intrusion of the common police into party discussions — these things reveal the truth. Those who say: "Politics first: Let him throw us into prison, as long as he pursues a correct policy," are very much mistaken.

It is untrue, a hundred times untrue that the end justifies the means. Justice is not made by iniquity, the world and men are not transformed by means of chains, loudspeakers crying out falsehoods, and vast agencies of intellectuals paid to cram people's head full of lies. Every end requires its own means, and an end is only obtained by the appropriate means. Though the socialist revolution may, in times of crisis, be forced to make use of the old weapons left by bourgeois society, afterwards it must find its own weapons. It can only progress by improving the material and moral condition of the masses. More personal well-being, more liberty, fewer lies, more dignity, more respect for humanity. The socialism which proceeds otherwise gives in to a sort of inner counterrevolution, discredits itself, and risks suicide.

The year 1928 plunged us headlong into that kind of socialism. Basic economic factors can plainly be seen to determine this evolution. Not that it was fatal; on the contrary, the Russian experience is all the more precious because it shows that economy can be governed, but that the consequences of a policy cannot be evaded. Let us consider the interrelation of cause and effect.

The party bureaus, beginning with the Politbureau, which is a veritable Directory,* lost years before deciding for industrialization. For years they let the kulaks — the rich peasants — make themselves comfortable. In order not to appear to give in to the Opposition, in order to retain power, the Politbureau rejected the suggestions for industrialization and deported those favoring a forced loan from the rich peasants — a suggestion offering obvious advantages.

They decapitated the old party, but immediately afterwards the government was without grain. Why should the peasant sell his wheat under such disadvantageous conditions? The cities lack bread. The army likewise. Stalin finds himself up a blind alley.

The grain that cannot be bought from the peasants must be taken from them. The Politbureau orders seizures by applying an unforeseen interpretation of Article 107 of the penal code, regarding the concealment of food supplies.

The peasants begin to hide their grain. The farmers sow less. What is the use of sowing if your harvest is going to be stolen?

By way of forcing the peasant to work, he is obliged to enter a cooperative supervised by the state, the *kolkhoz*.

If he refuses?

Those who refuse are called kulaks or agents of the kulaks, dispossessed of all they own and sent to the north with their families.

Many refuse. When partial collectivization has been introduced, it turns out that the peasants who have remained independent are much better off. As a last resort, the regime proclaims total collectivization — with enthusiasm, write Barbusse and several others — and the expropriation and mass deportation of the kulaks. This produces millions of dispossessed, expropriated peasants. . . .

In order to forestall the total ruin of agriculture, the most rapid industrialization is necessary. The five-year plan, revised and corrected to promise an output which six months before was considered out of the question, must be executed with enthusiasm.

And so it is. But the first consequence of the agrarian crisis, which in places degenerates into a scarcely concealed civil war, is to starve out the cities. Hastily, food cards are printed. From now on the workers receive rations so scanty as to be laughable. In November 1929, according to the official plac-

_____

*Body of five men who governed France after the downfall of the Convention, October 26, 1795 to November 9, 1799. Their regime was one of reaction against the revolution. — Translator.

ards in Moscow, the highest monthly ration for a worker belonging to a cooperative is:

three pounds of sugar	one and a half pounds of macaroni
two ounces of tea	one pound of herring
one pound of vegetable oil	one pound of household soap
six pounds of grits	

And that is the ration of the privileged proletariat in the
large centers.

The undernourishment of the workers diminishes the pro-
ductivity of labor. Rationing, the forced exchange rates, and
the inflation reduce the buying power of the paper ruble—in
which the workers receive their pay—to about 40 percent of
its buying power in 1926. The worker leaves the factory or
remains there only for form, and makes his actual living by
petty theft, small business deals and speculation. By reselling
a pair of stockings he earns more than by three days' labor.
The worker must be *forced* to work by draconic legislation.
In order to attach him to the industrial centers, internal passports are devised which deprive the population of the right to
move about freely, and make it possible to deport anyone
the administration wishes, without formality.

Before entering the *kolkhozes,* the peasants slaughter their
cattle. It seems just as well to gorge themselves with meat
for once in their lives and secretly sell the leather, as to give
their cattle to the state, with whose methods they are only too
familiar. The cattle disappear.

These years are a nightmare. Famine comes to the Ukraine,
the Black Lands, Siberia, to all the Russian granaries. Thousands of peasants flee across the frontiers to Poland, Rumania,
Persia, or China. They escape. A certain number of them are
killed attempting to cross the border. But the rest escape.

The death penalty is restored for good in the cities and in
the country. For the theft of a sheaf of wheat from a *kolkhoz:*
the death penalty. By virtue of the decree of August 7, 1932,
socialist property is declared sacred; its theft is punished by
death.

What can the five-year plan yield under these circumstances?
The population has been promised an era of abundance after
so many sacrifices. The fifth year of the plan is accompanied
by total famine.   Who is responsible? Name the culprits and
shoot them.

For years Stalin, the all-powerful, is silent (until the end
of 1933).

To find the guilty parties all you have to do is telephone

an order to the GPU. They will be arrested this very evening. Tomorrow they will have confessed, and the day after tomorrow they can be executed. After that, all you have to do is reprint the telegrams of enthusiastic approval, of admiring confidence, and of felicitations for the building of socialism that will pour in from all the capitals of the earth.

No meat nor canned goods? Professor Karatygin and forty-seven accomplices confess in secret session with the GPU to having disorganized the manufacture of canned goods and the meat supply for counterrevolutionary motives. And they are shot (1930).

The five-year plan encounters obstacles? It has been sabotaged by a secret "industrial party" collaborating with the French General Staff. Professor Ramzin (an agent provocateur) confesses. He is condemned to death, pardoned, rehabilitated, and rewarded (1930).

The people are not convinced? Nine old socialists confess to having conspired for French military intervention in the USSR under the directives of the Socialist International. What difference does it make that these directives are highly improbable and that the falsehood of their testimony is proved incontrovertibly? They have confessed. Ten years of imprisonment (1931).

Leningrad goes through a summer without either fruit or vegetables. Five managers of cooperatives are shot. But the following summers there is again no fruit and vegetables. . . .

Obviously no one can justify this regime by command — aside from those who, having brought the nation to such a pass, would inevitably be shot if they lost their power. The weight of its responsibilities renders the bureaucracy implacable. It must defend itself. Its entire policy since the consecration of its power has been aimed solely at the preservation of that power and has been dominated by fear and panic.

The Stalinist bureaucracy no longer pursues the policies of the working class, but its own policies. This is the inner significance of its acts.

Woe to anyone who raises his voice against the bureaucracy! Each year, prior to all holidays and congresses, thousands of suspected Oppositionists are arrested. The authentic Oppositionists have been imprisoned since 1928. Woe to him who says nothing. Silence is interpreted as evasion, as an attempt to elude crushing responsibilities. No. Under all circumstances the citizen must approve everything in a loud voice — everything, *everything!* Nothing remains but magnificent resolutions voted unanimously. And death sentences. The poets vote in verse in the newspapers.

Nothing can be expected from foreign socialists. They under-

stand too well. And what is happening can only be justified
by a revolutionary passion as blind as it is insincere. The Communist International announces in 1928 that "Germany, France,
Poland have entered upon a period of revolutionary upheavals."
Doriot invites the peasants to prepare "to take the land by force
of arms." Class against class. In Germany, where the Nazi
wave is mounting, the official doctrine of the CI is that fascism
will only be overcome over the dead body of the Social
Democracy. When in 1932 the Nazis obtain a plebiscite in
Prussia for the purpose of overthrowing Otto Braun's social
democratic cabinet, the Communist Party of Germany — on
Stalin's personal recommendation — joins forces with the Nazis,
and the *Rote Fahne* calls this the "Red plebiscite."

I have lived through what I describe. But I wish to quote
some unpublished or little known statements, whose absolute
veracity I can guarantee.[32] I am sure that no one will contest a single line. . . .

INDUSTRIALIZATION AND COLLECTIVIZATION

Life in a *kolkhoz*:

The members of the *kolkhoz* have for two months received
no pay for their labor, consisting of transporting wood and
feed. Fifty percent of the revenue goes to the *kolkhoz*
treasury, fifty percent for taxes and rent. What remains
for the workers? No one knows. The president pays himself several flour certificates each month and refrains from
all physical labor. "The first few months," he tells us, "the
members of the *kolkhoz* must live by their own resources."
But the poor have no reserves. They wear out their clothes
at work without compensation. All this lends credence to
the kulaks' assertion that a "new serfdom" is being instituted.

In a neighboring village, forty women have recovered
their cows by force, shut them up in the houses, and said
to the authorities of the rural soviet: "You can fire, but
you can't have our cows." However, the cattle are taken.
. . . It is hard to believe that such abominations are done
in the name of socialism. The rumor is circulating that
Zinoviev and Kamenev have been deported to the provinces. . . . (M. R. Letter written in April 1930).

In March 1930, Stalin authorized a certain number of peasants to leave the *kolkhozes*. His message finds fault with the local authorities for becoming "drunk with success. . . ."

> The *kolkhozes* are emptying. Eighty peasants in this hole-in-the-ground came to the public prosecutor to complain that they had been forced by violence to join the *kolkhoz*. Presidents of *kolkhozes* have been assassinated in the vicinity. Everywhere the women demand and take their cattle. . . . In the cities there is neither butter, meat, eggs, nor potatoes, and even the capitals are on microscopic rations. For a long time we have seen neither meat nor fish. During the last few days the cooperatives have at last received some horse sausage (Q. N. Letter written in April 1930).

A factory worker writes:

> They are squeezing us, and how! 25 percent increase in the productivity of labor and 1.9 percent increase in wages. For three years, wages have not varied, though production has very much increased. Five men to the brigade instead of six, without change of equipment. The system of bonuses is applied in such a way that, allowing for 20 to 30 percent a month, they should be paid every six months, but in reality no one hopes to receive any. We live on 55 rubles a month . . . (M., March 23, 1930).

On collectivization in Central Asia:

> The peasants receive minimal advances; the apportionment of the profits takes place at the end of the year. If the *kolkhoz* has made a profit, the salaries are not paid in entirety unless the sums paid into the collective capital are above the sum of the salaries. Otherwise, the *kolkhoznik* only receives a given percentage of his nominal salary. (See *Ruling of the Uzbekistan Kolkhoz Center.*) The peasants, collectivized by force, have no stimulus to work.
> . . . The peasants have replied to the forced collectivization by selling their possessions, sabotaging the work and revolting. A considerable rebellion broke out in one district of Sir Daria and lasted three weeks. . . .
> . . . The peasants say with right: "The Army is well fed and dressed; it will not support us . . ." (L. L., Letter written on March 27, 1930).

Another comrade writes that two hundred abandoned horses are wandering around near the village to which he has been deported. We hear of nothing but revolts, assassinations, outbreaks of rage and despair, deportations, mass migrations.

In a message to the government, the Abkhazes of the Southern Caucasus offer it all their possessions; with oriental politeness, they thank the government for all the benefits it has heaped upon them and ask only one favor: permission to emigrate to Turkey.

An American correspondent, utterly devoted to Stalin's interests, sets at two million the approximate number of those deported and exiled in 1929-1930 (*New York Times,* February 3, 1931). But the truth appears far worse if we realize that the dekulakization continued without let-up through the following years, and that the official figures vary between five and ten million in their estimate of the number of kulaks. . . . (In 1933, shortly after the end of the first five-year plan, the Rostov press, accidentally breaking through its forced silence, notes the mass deportation of three Cossack towns in the Kuban, totaling about 50,000 persons; and more than 100,000 inhabitants of the same region had preceded them on the road northward.) We can, therefore, assume that at least five million peasants, without distinction of age or sex, have been hunted from their homes and given over to undeserved misery or death. [33]

A Siberian exile writes:

I wish to relate what I have seen of the ousting of the kulaks in one region alone. First, we witnessed the arrival of 3,000 deported kulaks. Many of them were poor or middle peasants. Some of them had received decorations for bravery in the civil war, but their decorations had, of course, been taken from them. According to the plan, they were supposed to cut timber, but no arrangements had been made for them. The crowding in the barracks soon caused an epidemic of typhus. In the forests it was even worse. They were sent into the woods with their wives, I do not know why, in midwinter, without any warm clothing. . . .

They were preparing for a general revolt under the leadership of former soldiers. We succeeded in preventing this new calamity by persuading the authorities to abrogate the order sending them into the forests. . . .

All this closely resembles sabotage on an enormous scale.

A friend who has passed through a good many *kolkhozes* tells me that nothing remains of the old villages, and that a return to individual holdings would no longer be possible without terrible upheavals. About fifteen percent of the farmers are firmly for the *kolkhozes*. These are the young communists. They do everything; they work beyond human strength. The other peasants go into the *kolkhozes* because they cannot do otherwise, but they make sure to enter with empty hands. "From now on," they say, "we are state peasants. Just like workers . . . " (X., Letter written August 5, 1931).

The poor peasants are also treated as enemies:

The peasants' assemblies are being purged. A nearby soviet has just announced the expulsion of twenty poor peasants, some of whom are sincerely devoted to the regime. All are condemned as "agents of the kulaks." Their crime is that they have not always kept silent, that they have said their condition has grown worse, and asked if there would be another five-year plan. (The reporter said this question played into the hands of the kulaks.)*

This great drama of the Russian countryside is described in a remarkable literary document written, as it happens, by an official apologist: Sholokhov's novel *Cleared Land*.

Lest the mistakes and the crimes of the bureaucratic regime be imputed to socialism, we must here make a short digression on a point of doctrine. Socialism does not involve this treatment of the peasants, but is, on the contrary, opposed to it. The socialist peasant policy is quite different, and the proletarian parties of the future will draw profit from the Russian experience, as an example not to follow. (It is, however, by no means impossible that a fascist bureaucracy in the service of finance capital, plunged by circumstances into a grain shortage, should apply the Stalinist methods to small farm holdings. . . .)

Lenin tirelessly repeats: "Do not force the peasants. . . ." The state founded by the Bolsheviks calls itself a state of workers and peasants: that is its official title. Though sanctioning the fight against the rural bourgeoisie as against any other bourgeoisie, Lenin's recommendation as passed by the Second

---

* The Russian **Bulletin of the Opposition,** appearing in Paris, has published a great many such letters. — V. S.

Congress of the CI was that this bourgeoisie must not be expropriated immediately after the seizure of power.[34] He writes:

> Engels emphasized that socialists have no thought of
> expropriating the small farmers, but rather seek to show
> them by force of example the advantages of socialized
> and mechanized agriculture.

And elsewhere, in one of his fundamental speeches on the
NEP, introduced as a policy of conciliation with the rural
population:

"The very principle of our dictatorship is to maintain the
alliance of the proletariat with the peasantry, in order that
the proletariat may retain power."[35]

Trotsky, in *The Revolution Betrayed,* emphasizes the part
played by improvisation — owing either to ineptitude or the
force of circumstances — in collectivization. A few months before proclaiming total collectivization, the Politbureau conceived
that the process would have to take many years.

. . . From his exile in Constantinople, Trotsky never ceased
to protest severely against what he considered a "fatal economic
adventure." No more than you can build a transatlantic liner
by assembling hundreds or thousands of fishing smacks —
he wrote with bitter irony — can you create modern, large-
scale agriculture by forcing small farmers to pool together
their ploughs, their oxen, and their chickens. . . . True socialist collectivization must be brought to the farmer by showing
him the unquestionable advantage of its mechanization and
planning.

Take care not to remind anyone of these elementary Marxist
truths. It will not be good for your health.

Let us return once more to the Soviet Union. From a letter
from Moscow, April 1933:

> A strike just occurred in a printing plant employing
> from 500 to 600 workers. Causes: during forced stoppages
> owing to lack of paper, the workers received only 75 per-
> cent of their wages, and bad food at the cooperative. The
> communists also stopped work and will be judged by the
> Control Commission. Several functionaries were immediate-
> ly dismissed and all the workers' demands acceded to;
> three of the "ringleaders" are in prison.
>   . . . Panic reigns as a consequence of the distribution
> of passports. About 30 percent of the inhabitants have

been refused passports for Moscow and expect to be ordered to leave the city by the first of May.

. . . Last winter was just as hard as the winter of 1919. Typhus raged. In the small stations we saw the sick abandoned, devoured by lice. Railroad tickets for certain regions quarantined for typhoid were refused. This was the case for North Caucasus and Central Asia, where there is more than typhus: in those places the uprisings have assumed the proportions of a local civil war.

. . . A communist writer said to me recently: "Why do I no longer write? What would you have me write at the present time? I'm only waiting for a chance to be sent to the Pamir, or to the Arctic Ocean on an icebreaker. That's the best you can do at a time like this."

Impressions of the Ukraine at the same period:

Kharkov has appreciably grown. There are many new factories and cooperative houses. Thousands of persons, however, spend their evenings without light and almost without heat. Entire sections of the city lack electricity. The movies are closed, the dwelling houses in darkness. And this goes on for whole weeks. No oil, no candles, total darkness. Only the bureaucrats, the lucky bastards, have bad kerosene lamps. There is no oil, though the production of petroleum at Baku has increased. No electricity, though the Dneprostroi is finished. It is terribly depressing. The same in the other cities. The people live stupidly in a bestial despair. The contrast between production and consumption is overwhelming. With more machines we live not better, but worse.

I have seen the Dneprostroi. It is truly a splendid work of human intelligence and strength. Beautiful as a toy, clean, resplendent, magnificent. Of the four completed units, three are inactive; the factories for which they are supposed to furnish the power do not yet exist. That's planning for you. And if the electric plant is clean and well-kept, the workers' quarters are quite otherwise. The newspapers harp on the fact that a village formerly located there has grown to a city of 70,000 inhabitants. They describe the clubs and show pictures of the workers' dwellings. Is all this a lie? No, it's all true. But what they don't say is that only a small minority of the workers live under tolerable conditions. The others live in squalid barracks in darkness, filth, cold, and undernourishment. Their faces are peaked; expressing not discontent but utter despair. It cannot last long. . . .

. . . Lice, on which Lenin once declared war, have returned in numbers. Filthy crowds fill the stations; men, women, and children in heaps, waiting for God knows what trains. They are chased out, and they return without money or tickets. They board any train they can and stay on it until they are put off. They are silent and passive. Where are they going? Just in search of bread, potatoes, or work in the factories where the workers are less badly fed. . . . Bread is the great mover of these crowds. What can I say of the thefts? People steal everywhere, everywhere. . . .

The leaders demand optimism. "We have seen hard times before." All the motions they put forward are passed unanimously. Eight communists out of ten have plenty of doubts, but they vote just the same. In answer to any reproaches, they say: "What good would it do for me to go to rot in Siberia?"

The wife of a capitulator who had been arrested tells me that she said to the prosecutor: "Why do you torment him? He has given up all opposition long ago and does his work as best he can. . . ." The GPU agent's only answer was to advise her to get divorced. . . .

A few words on repressions from a letter written in February 1933:

Kirov, speaking in Leningrad to the active members of the party, said: "We shall be pitiless, and not only against the communists who engage in counterrevolutionary activity [that is to say, Oppositionists], but also those lacking in firmness in the factory and the villages and who fail to carry out the plan. Four hundred members of the party have already been sent to the Solovetski Islands."

. . . Arrests in the right wing of the party are continuing. A large number of functionaries of the Commissariat of Agriculture have just been arrested, accused of sabotage. Several of these belonged to the government. Konor, the People's Vice-Commissar for Agriculture, and Wolfe and Kovarsky, members of the Council of the Commissariat, were, it appears, at the head of the conspiracy. They are accused of having had relations with the Ukrainian nationalists in Poland. It is possible that there were traitors in the Commissariat of Agriculture, but this affair seems to have been concocted out of loose ends. Konor, a native of Galicia, became a Bolshevik during the war, took part in the civil war and some years ago, I believe, sympathized with the Left Opposition. . . . No one believes these accusations. Everyone thinks the chief is preparing a trial of ostensible saboteurs of agriculture by way of setting an example. . . .

There was no trial. Konor, Kovarsky, Wolfe, and thirty-two other functionaries and agronomists were executed without trial in Moscow in the first days of March 1933.

OUTLAWED

This brings us to the question of repression. The entire system has rested on repression since the day when the leaders began to be selected with the aid of the GPU. There is little to be said on the subject of freedom of speech and of thought. All the socialists of all shades of opinion, without any exception, are deported or in prison. All the anarchists and syndicalists likewise. All the communist Oppositionists. Official thought tolerates not the slightest shadow or suspicion of criticism. After 1930 mere suspects are persecuted. Old men long retired from all political life, but who may once have been anarchists, socialists, or communist Oppositionists, disappear one night, and many months later we hear that they have arrived at the Ust-Pechora concentration camp, or that they have been deported to the tundras of the Yenisei.

Those suspected of political heresy are especially numerous within the ranks of the party. An awkward word, reticence on some point, a moment's hesitation (it may have occurred many years before, but some informer remembers it), even silence may suffice. The suspect disappears. The prisons are full of them. Four to five thousand Oppositionists were arrested between 1928 and 1930. The number of suspects is even higher. After 1934 and the assassination of Kirov by a young Leningrad communist, communists and other suspects were herded into captivity by tens and more probably hundreds of thousands. With this labor, excluded from the benefits of the Labor Code, canals are dug, strategic roads built. Several hundred thousands of prisoners worked on the Baltic-White Sea

Canal. How many of them died in the process? The official writers do not tell us.

The Soviet Union has the vastest concentration camps in the world. Those of Kem-Solovetski (White Sea), Karaganda (Central Asia), the mouth of the Pechora and others, occupy entire districts. There are concentration camps everywhere, including forced-labor camps, dungeons, lumber camps, mines. There are filthy holes and model camps—attractive reform colonies for the edification of foreign investigators and movie-goers. (What, indeed, is simpler than to reform the criminal? Give the highwayman and the pick-pocket well-remunerated work, a good shelter, and intelligent amusements, and nine times out of ten you will obtain the desired results, for the excellent reason that they never would have stolen if they had always been placed in satisfactory living conditions.) As for the politicals, they are not exhibited. Those who resist and die in hunger strikes, defending their dignity — the one thing that is left to them — those men are never seen.

The reader desiring detailed information on this chapter of Soviet life will pardon me for referring him to my book *Destin de la Revolution* (American title, *Russia: Twenty Years After*). Here I shall limit myself to quoting a few authentic documents offering glimpses of the realities.

The repression is based on provocation:

> The Central Committee is growing increasingly more panicky and reacts by persecuting us. It is difficult to find words to describe the extent of the persecution. . . . Mass arrests. They arrest people for a word interpreted as signi-fying sympathy for the Opposition, for a few words spoken in the factory at the meetings for self-criticism. Hundreds of nonparty workers have been accused of opposition and imprisoned in Butirky prison; many have been deported, and new ones keep arriving. The art of provocation was highly developed last year, but today it assumes gigantic proportions. Provocateurs are encountered in prison, in exile, everywhere. The special task of the provocateurs in exile is to demoralize the colonies of exiles by exhorting some to capitulate, by denouncing others to the authorities as recalcitrants. The recalcitrants will soon be sent to dif-ferent spots or locked up. . . . The exiles are constantly submitted to search, arrests, transfers, deprived of tobacco, and so on forever (Letter from Moscow, May 5, 1930).

It is the same, of course, in the entire "sixth part of the world."

Kharkov, August 3, 1930. Here everything goes on as in the past: arrests, imprisonment, deportations for us, congresses where everything is voted unanimously for the bureaucrats. . . . Quite a number were just arrested. Bogdanov, of the machine shop, was elected by the workers as president of the shop committee despite the intervention of a party big shot. The GPU stepped in with Article 58 and settled that affair.

From a letter from Central Asia, August 1930:

Our godfathers [the GPU] are getting ready for the Sixteenth Party Congress: There is nothing but nocturnal visits, searching parties, arrests, transfers. Avoyan, who had been deported to Bukhara, has now been sent to the Verkhne-Uralsk isolator; Maria Joffe, on the other hand, has arrived in Bukhara; at Rubtsov five of our comrades out of ten were locked up; three exiles were arrested at Kzyl-Orda in the middle of July; six in Kazalinsk. Similar news arrives from Biisk, Kansk, Shimkent, Orenburg, Alma Ata, Omsk, Tomsk, Slavgorod. Provocation wherever you turn. No one has work. We have to get along with the 15 rubles alloted by the GPU, while the absolute minimum for living is 60 rubles. We are firm, however.

The exiles they want to kill are transferred unceasingly from one end of the backwoods to the other, deprived of work, harassed for years.

Just before the congress, a number of Oppositionists, considered too firm, were transferred into the filthiest holes. Nina Stern was transferred from Uralsk to Kara-Tube where she is in danger of literally starving and where there have been cases of plague. One of our people, arriving in Turi-Kul, found a whole colony of his comrades there. Several have just capitulated, for resistance had become physically impossible. We are like mice for the cats to play with. But that is no reason to let ourselves be impressed and to imagine that the cat is the strongest thing in the world. . . .

T. gave in after two years of exile. They got him, he said. "I am an invalid," he writes. "My nerves are broken, I have a stomach ulcer and scurvy [acquired in prison]. Those are the chief reasons for my capitulation, though in addition I am pessimistic." The workers here are depressed: the prices go up, food is lacking. The disappearance of silver money is significant. . . .

To give in, to capitulate, is to renounce all thought, to sign a dictated form declaring one's approval and admiration of the "line laid down by the brilliant leader." . . . It is to place oneself at the disposal of the authorities for the purpose of observing, propagandizing, and denouncing the others — the stronger comrades who are holding out. To capitulate and retain any dignity is not easy: one is considered doubly suspect. . . . One capitulator writes:

> I am permitted to work in the factory, but I make only 50 rubles a month. The Committee has twice refused me readmission into the party. The reason is distrust; they doubt my sincerity. My former Oppositionist friends avoid me like the plague. Party members look on me askance. If I make the slightest criticism, they say: "You're backsliding." If I say something is well done, I am trying to "dissimulate and bore from within." I have decided to say nothing, but now I am accused of "finding fault by silence" and "declining my responsibilities." To tell the truth, I feel like a leper. . . .

True no doubt, but the fate of those who hold out is often worse.

> Our exiles lack everything: they are literally exposed to cold and hunger. V. wrote me yesterday: "They want to starve us into submission, but we shall not capitulate."
> We take up collections, but it is extremely dangerous (November 1932).
> Katya Kh. was in Chardyr with a one-year-old infant. In all her letters she implored the comrades not to let her little one die of hunger. When she had completed her three years' exile, she was sent to Central Asia with a convoy of criminals and given 50 kopeks a day for her subsistence. I must tell you that a pound of bread costs between two and three rubles. Elsewhere, the same picture: the situation among the exiles is frightful.
> Many of them are sick. Solntsev is in prison with scurvy. He has completed his term, but they don't let him out. His wife suggested that he ask to be deported, but he absolutely refused.
> Eleazar Solntsev, one of our most capable young militants, died of a hunger strike at Novosibirsk hospital in January 1936.
> Three comrades have been let out of prison after a hunger strike, but one of them died.

Mussia Magid was set free and deported in a convoy with common-law prisoners to Minusinsk after having spent six months in bed in a prison cell. She is now in bed again. She is courageous, but she writes to her parents that she does not expect to see them again. Gayev has returned from Verkhne-Uralsk prison to Moscow: he has gone blind as a result of pernicious anemia. Vladimir Kossior is in Minusinsk . . . (Letter written November 1932).[36]

Men *disappear* in the prisons.

Two hundred and fifty of our people are in the Verkhne-Uralsk isolator. After a protest on the part of the prisoners, Yanushevsky, considered to be a ringleader, was sent to Moscow, shut up in the inner prison, and, the rumors say, condemned to ten years of concentration camp. As collective protests are not tolerated, this is what is done: one comrade raises a protest, and the others individually declare their agreement with him. That is what Yanushevsky did. Since then nothing has been heard of him, and many months have passed. The Schwalbach brothers, one of whom was seriously ill with tuberculosis, have likewise disappeared after a long stay in the inner prison of the Moscow GPU.

It is true that in the cities there is much more "disappearing" and for the same reasons. . . .

Do not think that I have chosen exceptional statements or unusual occurrences. From among a heap of documents, I have taken more or less at random a few lines of those which seem to me most characteristic for their commonplaceness. Whoever is in the least acquainted with Russian life will back me up. The letters I have quoted are several years old, because *we have ceased to receive any letters*. The system has been perfected, nothing gets through any more; but the situation has grown much worse. To these statements we must therefore add a large coefficient of cruelty and ferocity. In the last few years the repressions have not ceased to increase in scope and in brutality.

On prison life:

One of our comrades used to say that we shall serve as manure to fertilize the earth in which after us new human harvests of the revolution will spring up. The state of mind has much improved. We hope for a change. We are all working to increase our knowledge, to learn languages, especially German. Endless discussions on cosmology, space, time, mechanics, Marxism, the Rightist peril. The censorship permits nothing of our intellectual life to leak out. Even the number of comrades who can communicate with one another in prison is extremely limited. We have gone through several hunger strikes: after the first, we obtained twelve letters instead of four per month. This strike was very long, and several of the comrades came out of it seriously ill. The second strike was a protest against brutality; in it we also refused all communication with the outside world. Our nerves are tense. We are almost at the end of our strength. There is no doubt that the socialists issued from the czar's prisons in better shape than we shall be in when we leave Stalin's isolators (Letter written June 1930).

At the end of the summer of 1931 the brutalities in the Verkhne-Uralsk isolator culminated in the attempted assassination of an imprisoned comrade named Essayan, who was wounded by a bullet in the chest. Thirty Oppositionists went on an eighteen-day hunger strike. The authorities tried to feed them by force. Thirty came down with scurvy. A delegation of twelve Bolshevik-Leninist prisoners, invited to a conference by the authorities, was kidnapped and taken to an unknown destination.

In 1933 a vast hunger strike occurred in the prisons with a certain success, in protest against the automatic doubling of terms. The GPU (today the Commissariat of Public Safety — only the name has changed) hands out penalties of three years hard labor without sentence or statement of cause, as an administrative measure. If, at the expiration of his term, the Oppositionist is not convinced of the excellence of the regime, he is given a two-year supplementary term. After completing their five years, a few dozen old communists obtained the right to be freed *and exiled* by threatening to let themselves all die of hunger. . . . They would have carried out their threat.

Several months later, they were all arrested in exile and, as an administrative measure, condemned to five years of imprisonment. Such is the fate of my friends: Gregory Yakovin, Fedor Dingelstedt, Vassili Pankratov, Chanaan Pevzner, and many others. Socialist thought has had no more stoical heroes.

One more touch:

Within the GPU as elsewhere, fear and confusion reign.

No one trusts anyone else. At the least suspicion, often unjustified — for instance, for having been polite to an arrested Oppositionist or for having been too "easy" in the course of a house search — men are dismissed. The least mistake leads to arrests. The least complaisance toward the Opposition is punished by death. I have just received confirmation of the fact which I had previously reported: I have learned from an absolutely reliable source that the warden of Tomsk prison, who had consented to delivering a letter to Sosnovsky, was shot.

I have said nothing of the suicides, the assassinations, the secret executions. There would be too much to say. I have abridged, but I can prove everything.

REMINISCENCES

I spent eighty-five days in a cell in the inner GPU prison without reading or occupation of any sort, without news of my people. I spent seventy of those days in total solitude, without even taking the air in the grey courtyard reserved for the more tractable prisoners. Now they have shipped me 2000 kilometers away. A good comrade and I almost died of hunger; we met in the cellar of a prison in Samara.

He: Right communist, former secretary of such and such a district, took part in the civil war.

I: Left communist, former, etc. . . .

The sky was wonderful after my imprisonment.

I live in a nice tumbledown old house on the hill, with its back to the plain. The steppe extends infinitely as far as Kara Kum, Altai, Kamchatka. The horizon is as beautiful as the sea. Across the way, the ruins of a poor suburb. Above me the sky is unforgettably pure. Around me the people are famished, alcoholic, malarial. Good people, all in all. Wretchedly poor. It is five minutes walk to the city with its three movie houses. The place would be inhabitable, it would have its charm like any corner of the Russian soil, if not for the regime, the police supervision, and all the rest of it.

This is a quiet sector of the exile. No persecution. Several comrades have work. I have none. I write, I write. I must create, work in order not to go mad, in order to fulfill my task here on earth; to be useful, to leave behind me a little emotion and thought. To work is to resist. For there is a soul in all work.

A friend has just arrived here from prison. (And prison is awaiting him, but does it not await us all?) "Do you know," he asked me, "that Shevtshenko* was deported right here to Orenburg about 1850 and forbidden to write? He used to go out into the steppe and scribble his poems. He hid them in the sole of his boots. . . . Where will you hide your books?"

And there's something in that. . . . The hardest is this sensation of slow suffocation. In eighteen months not a letter has come.

My comrades and the population hereabouts believe that we shall never be released. For we shall never give in. We shall never abandon our communist thought. We shall not worship the gravedigger of the revolution. We shall not approve the boundless misery of all those who toil, the rebirth of privilege, the stifling of every living word. So much the worse for us. They will not hesitate to shoot us if things go badly. God knows what means of getting rid of us they will think up. But we know they will find something. Already, without any special effort on their part, one of us is wasting away of bone tuberculosis, another is sent into a concentration camp, others disappear. . . .

Vassili Pankratov disappeared. He was a *man*. Well-balanced, strong, smiling, despite all he had been through. Three years of imprisonment. Two years additional for firmness of character. And it is true that no one was ever firmer. Before this, he went through the whole civil war. Served with the navy in Kronstadt; was in the uprising against the Provisional Government; fought in the Red Army. Former vice-president of the GPU in Transcaucasia, Left communist. His wife had waited for him for five years. He had been released some months before and she had accompanied him in exile. Now they were going to have a child. Less than six months after his liberation and deportation, he was arrested without known reason, and disappeared. He was in prison in Verkhne-Uralsk for five years. The child was born in our midst, fatherless. What means will they think up of assassinating Pankratov in prison? Will they reduce him to a fatal hunger strike? I wonder; for revolutionists of his stamp, men of conviction, incorruptible and loyal to the death, bear within them the

---

*Shevtshenko, poet and painter, the national pride of the Ukraine. A very impressive monument has just been erected to him at Kiev. — V. S.

living condemnation of the regime, and it is obvious that the regime cannot let them live. . . .

Chanaan Pevzner disappeared. The same convictions, the same cast of character. He too had been imprisoned, but only for four years (after two years exile) because of sickness. He had returned from a campaign in the Far East with ten bullets in his body and a disjointed arm; all its bones broken and hanging like a rag. He too went through life smiling. He was possessed of a merciless insight. He was the most persistent in saying: "The main thing is not to harbor any illusions on our fate." After the Kirov business, they arrested him as he was leaving the hospital after an attack of scarlet fever. . . . Is he alive and, if so, in what prison?

I am abridging the story, I repeat. I name only these two men, my comrades and brothers. I chanced to be a witness to their faith, their probity, their disappearance. I narrowly escaped the same fate. My strict duty is to accuse the men who persecuted them.

These revolutionists are in a curious situation now that Lenin's generation is being done away with. They had been too long in captivity (about eight years) for them to have been accused of the plot. It is well known that there is no possibility of extracting obliging confessions from them, and that they may on no account be permitted to speak at a public trial. . . . How will they be done away with?

As for confessions, I know by experience how they are dictated and manufactured. During my so-called "questioning," which was in reality nothing better than an inquisition, I was asked to confess, but I didn't know what I was intended to say. I was curious to know how they would go about informing me what they wanted me to confess. When they considered me ripe — that is to say, sufficiently demoralized by solitary confinement, idleness, and threats — an examining magistrate very coldly informed me that I was facing a very long confinement in any case, and that I could obtain an attenuation of my sentence only by confirming the confessions of my sister-in-law, Anita Russakova, which he was going to read to me. . . .

Thereupon he began to read to me in a loud voice a curious document, not one word of which was true, containing the names and addresses of persons totally unknown to me. I immediately understood that little Anita was lost: whether she had been made to sign this dime novel or whether it was attributed to her without her having signed it, she could never again be set free; and I knew that I myself was lost, for after

they had thus compromised themselves in my presence they
would naturally have to get rid of me. An address — unknown
to me — which could have been that of a military man, made
me think that they were going to accuse me of high treason
and shoot me. In that case, I had nothing more to lose. I cut
the pig short. "You are causing your own ruin," he said. "I
don't care," I answered, "but that's enough. I won't have anything to do with your lies." I was saved, and Anita was released.

I demanded, without obtaining it, a meeting with her. The
investigation was cut short; their forgery was forgotten. Passing
through Moscow last April, on my way out of Russia, I hoped
to see Anita once more. I learned that she had been arrested.
Again? For what reason? This woman had never belonged to
any political grouping. All those who know her are aware
that her character is beyond reproach. She is timorous. No
reason was given for the insane penalty of five years deportation to Vyatka; an administrative measure.

Nothing is ever published on this sort of affair. There is no
one to defend us. No one to help us. We are simply strangled
in the dark.

THE PERSECUTION OF WOMEN

I remember a young woman whom I met in Zinoviev's
room in Petrograd in 1920. She was delicate, blonde, pretty.
She had an air of aristocratic refinement that was conspicuous
among the coarse faces of the time. She was the head of an information service. With her I often saw the Assyrian beard of
her husband, Ambassador Joffe — Adolf Abramovich to his
friends — an old revolutionist while still young, having behind
him arrests, escapes, all sort of exploits. He had played a
certain part in the German revolution of 1918. He had signed
the peace treaties with Estonia and Poland. Lenin sent him to
China and Japan: to China to win over Sun Yat-sen; to Japan
to confirm the peace. I met him once in Vienna, where he
politely swept out of his path the Balkan conspirators who
were proposing to him all sorts of *coups d'etat.* . . . Maria
Mikhailovna had a son. . . . Sick and harassed by a covert
persecution (for he had always belonged to the revolutionary
Left of the party), Joffe blew out his brains on November
16, 1927, at his desk beneath a large portrait of Lenin. He

left a testament in the form of a letter addressed to Trotsky. In the next room, filled with comrades moving about among scattered toys, sat Maria Mikhailovna with compressed lips. . . . Before killing himself, Joffe wrote:

> More than thirty years ago, I adopted the philosophy that human life has meaning only in so far as it is put into the service of something infinite, which for us is humanity. . . .
> . . . I have lived in accordance with this meaning of life: work and the good and humanity. Even in the years of imprisonment. . . .

No longer able to fight, forced by sickness to suicide:

> My death is a protest against those who have led the party into a situation in which it can in no way react against shame and disgrace. . . .

Some months later, the widow of this great servant of the revolution, now working on children's literature in the state publishing house, attends a party meeting at which the names of all those she loves and whose ideas she shares are covered with filth. She takes the floor. Two days later she is arrested and deported to Alma Ata, then to Bukhara. After three years, she was once again deported for another three. She showed herself inflexibly faithful to her revolutionary principles and her memories. At the end of this second term she was imprisoned for attempting to organize a demonstration of solidarity for comrades who had fallen into the deepest misery — an act characterized as counterrevolutionary. Her lease to deportation was renewed for the third time. In the meantime her child had succumbed to its privations.

The day after the Zinoviev case, the news agencies reported the suicide of Maria Joffe. I refused to believe it, yet it is possible; not as an act of despair, but as a last act of resistance to the reaction. How shall we ever know what has become of Maria Joffe?

Another woman, Eva Broido, a social democrat (Menshevik), went to Russia illegally in 1927 for her party. She was denounced by an agent provocateur and imprisoned in Suzdal for three years. When she was released, if you can call it that, she was deported for five years to Tashkent. At the end of these five years, she was sent for five more years to Ulala on the Mongolian border, a hundred kilometers from the nearest railroad station. . . . Eva Broido is almost sixty years of age. She has been a militant socialist since 1890, and saw the inside of many prisons under the czar; in 1904 she took part in the struggles of the exiles in Yakutsk, for which she received a number of years at hard labor. . . .

In many countries there are women's organizations, dedicated to socialism, peace, or other generous ideals. . . . Is it possible that they are ignorant of the fate of Maria Joffe, Eva Broido, Irina Kakhovskaya, Maria Spiridonova, Maria Ivanova, Dora Zak, Alexandra Bronstein, Zeinl Muehsam?* And if these cases are known to them, what are we to think of their silence?

TERROR AND ECONOMIC RECOVERY

In this tense atmosphere, in this vast country whose rulers attach so little value to human life, how can we be astonished at an isolated murder? Kirov, a member of the Politbureau and Stalin's representative in Leningrad, was assassinated on December 1, 1934, by a young communist, Leonid Nikolayev. The terrorist explained his act in written declarations which were *neither published nor read in any public trial*. Fourteen young communist comrades of his were shot after a secret trial. *One hundred and sixteen persons* having nothing whatever to do with this crime, *and who had been arrested previous to it*, were shot. The world looked on without apparent emotion. The intellectual "friends of the Soviet Union" approved or were silent, not suspecting that by their silence they were preparing themselves for a bitter awakening. Liberal academicians and *literati*, the defenders of culture were silent. How can they now feel justified in defending the life of an Edgar Andre or a Thaelmann?

A clumsy attempt is made to implicate Trotsky in this act of individual terror. The GPU chiefs in Leningrad are severely condemned for having known of the preparation of the crime and not prevented it. This constitutes an official admission of provocation. All of a sudden, Stalin has all his silenced opponents in the party implicated for moral complicity. Zinoviev, Kamenev, Bakayev, Feodorov, Yevdokimov[37] are condemned

---

*Yes, the wife of Eric Muehsam, the libertarian poet assassinated by the Nazis in a German concentration camp, is in prison in the USSR. — V. S.

to long terms of imprisonment with confiscation of their property, that is to say, of their personal archives (correspondence with Lenin and political documents; this was assuredly one of the aims of the trial). Their political associates are sent to concentration camps by the thousands. Men who had formerly been known to profess revolutionary opinions are deported in droves. The Trotskyists who had been exiled on their release from prison are again imprisoned. The purge of the population of Leningrad (by imprisonment and deportation) includes between 80,000 and 100,000 victims. And that is in 1935, a year of economic recovery. . . . If the bureaucracy were not aware of its unpopularity, if it did not have so bad a conscience before the people, the police regime would be relaxed in a year like this. But the bureaucracy is dominated by fear.

Faced with the destruction of at least half the cattle and of more than half the horses, Stalin understood and changed his line. First the *kolkhozes* were authorized to trade for their own account. Little by little, small peasant property, including a small piece of land, a cow, a horse, was restored within the *kolkhoz*. The *kolkhozes* were promised the right to grow rich. . . . Grain reappeared.

At the beginning of 1935, food cards were suppressed, bread was sold freely by the state at 50 kopeks for a pound of gray bread. Now wages, however low, have a real value because they have an equivalent in merchandise. The worker earning a hundred rubles a month earns in reality 200 pounds of gray bread. He can live. Millions of workers earn no more than that. The average wage varies from 150 to 170 rubles depending on the locality, but the most common wage is, of course, far below the average. The country experiences a tremendous relief. It has risen from the depths. Things are at last on the upgrade. Faces are more cheerful.

The USSR enters the League of Nations, whose imperialist hypocrisy and permanent bankruptcy it had hitherto denounced. Russia becomes a great military power, in aviation perhaps the first in the world. We learn that the five-year plan has first and foremost been a rearmament plan. We learn with dismay that the Soviet state has been spending on tanks, five-motored bombers, autogiros, motorized artillery, marshals' stars, and the creation of a military aristocracy; all it has taken not from the prosperity, but from the penury of the masses. And this is madness, for its weakness will now be greater than its strength. The mightiest army in the world has behind it the most wretched and dissatisfied hinterland.

One thing leads to another. Here again fear is the chief explanation. During the years of famine and agrarian troubles,
1930-1935, the Soviet Union was on the verge of ruin. The
leaders sought by means of armaments to compensate for its
inner weakness.

THE BRILLIANT AND BELOVED LEADER

The famine is over. War has been avoided. The Soviets are
rewarded by the friendship of the French. The USSR reinforces
the League of Nations. "The crisis of world capitalism is
easing," Stalin declares.

He speaks frequently, shows himself to impassioned crowds—
carefully selected as you may well imagine—lunches with M.
Laval and informs him of the end of communist opposition
to militarism in France; lunches with Mr. Eden and sets his
mind at rest as to agitation in India; has his picture taken
with Romain Rolland, ascetic and thoughtful, meditating on
an encomium of Yagoda, the man of firing squads and concentration camps. . . . *

Stalin proclaims the happiness of the people, distributes decorations, phonographs, watches, with both hands and has his
picture taken kissing little girls of all the old races of Asia.
Father of the people. Poets, writers, orators, tractor mechanics,
Turkoman shepherds, Mongol ploughmen, Georgian aviators,
Uzbek schoolchildren have all run out of epithets for him. The
widows of dead aviators thank him, the entire press is nothing
but praises for the "beloved leader," "the wisest and greatest
of all ages." He is "brilliant," "beloved as the firstborn child,"
"radiant as the sun." And they print nothing else. Everything
revolves around the new Imperator cult. And never will the
paean of praise attain a higher pitch of exaltation than the
day after the leader has massacred his oldest comrades in
struggle, the men who had worked with Lenin. The totalitarian
press functions to perfection.

With his low forehead and coarse mustache, invariably clad
in an inelegant uniform without decoration, he looks and talks
like an ill-tempered noncommissioned officer. Joseph Vissariono-

---

*The Soviet press published this piece. . . . Many readers of **Jean-
Christophe** were astounded to read it. Was it worth living so long
and fine a life only to arrive at that?— V. S.

vich Djugashvili, a Georgian, born in Tiflis in 1879, the son
of a shoemaker; attended a seminary that turned out a good
many revolutionists; socialist and Bolshevik since the party's
beginnings, engaged in illegal activity in the Caucasus from
1898 to 1917, deported five times and escaped four. The revolution found him in the far north at Turukhansk. Stalin means
"made of steel," and that he is. Like a dagger. After the defeated
revolution of 1905, he became a terrorist, directing brilliant
expropriations and other acts of terrorism (since then he permitted to die in exile and without care his best friend of those
days, Kote Tsintsadze, an Oppositionist). Obscure and devoted
in 1917, he played a conspicuous part in the defense of
Tsaritsyn — today Stalingrad — along with Voroshilov and
Yegorov, today marshals. Lenin appreciated him sufficiently
to mistrust him a good deal and fear him a little. "He lacks
the most elementary honesty," he said. He attained to power
by intrigue in the bureaus and congresses, first siding with
Zinoviev, Kamenev, Rykov, Tomsky, and Bukharin against
Trotsky; then with Rykov, Tomsky, and Bukharin against
Zinoviev and Kamenev; then with Voroshilov, Kalinin, Ordjonikidze against Rykov, Tomsky, and Bukharin; and now
sole master through the murder or exile of all the leaders
of the revolution and the total destruction of the party which
made possible the years from 1917 to 1923.

His intellectual production is painfully wanting. Trotsky said
of him: "He is the greatest mediocrity in our party." He believes
in his mission. Perhaps the only one to believe in it; he has
shut himself up within the innermost spheres of hell. Though
intrepid, he lives in fear. Crafty, he lives on suspicion. Today
he ordains assassination, tomorrow apotheosis. What will it
be the next day?

ASSASSINATION

On August 19, 1936, the sixteen defendants in the Zinoviev-
Kamenev-Ivan Smirnov trial appeared before the supreme
military tribunal; on the twenty-fourth they were condemned
to death, and on the twenty-fifth, executed. They had confessed
(except Smirnov, who in the main was silent, and Holtzmann,
who only made confessions that were obviously false in
order to give the game away) what, in the interests of the

party, they had agreed to confess at the leader's demand. They understood too late that they had been tricked. [38]

Nothing is ever known of executions in Russia. But it seems that this time emotion pierced the mystery, for the large newspapers — outside of Russia, of course — ran a story which, for a number of reasons, presents a striking air of probability. I do not hesitate to state that it is in all likelihood true. . . .

. . . Kamenev was permitted to speak with his family. He received his wife [Trotsky's sister], his niece, and his daughter. His family was astonished to see "the mask of death" on his face. In a spent, weary voice, Kamenev said to them: "I shall probably go on a long voyage. I feel sick. The doctor took my pulse yesterday: it was between 58 and 60. If I die, do not think badly of those who judged me. They know what they are doing. . . ."

They had judged under orders; they too were serving the party. And he who had given the order, however criminal he might be, nonetheless symbolized the revolution. . . .

Kamenev was shot first. He did not resist, offered no complaint. He left his cell in silence and as if in a dream descended into the execution cellar. After the first revolver shot, fired apparently from behind, he let out an "ah!" of stupefaction and fell. He was still alive. Lieutenant Vasiukov, who was present, cried out in a hysterical voice: "Finish him," and gave the dying man a kick with his boot. A second bullet in the head finished Kamenev. . . .

Thus died the real leader of the Bolshevik fraction of the 1912 Duma, the first president of the Executive Committee of the Soviets in 1917, Lenin's sole heir, and, in addition, one of the most learned writers of contemporary Russia.

Smirnov, who had refused to sign an application for pardon, was the only one to preserve his calm and courage until the end. When, on leaving his cell, he saw the escort, he understood. He asked for a sheet of paper and said: "We have deserved this for our unworthy attitude at the trial. I conducted myself shamefully at the trial. I want to die like a revolutionist." Smirnov went down after Kamenev. . . .

Thus died the "Lenin of Siberia."

Zinoviev was in solitary confinement on the first floor of the GPU prison. After having been the first to sign the petition for pardon, he went to sleep. Though it was warm, he was shivering. He had on flannel drawers and woolen socks. They awakened him at one in the morning. He sat up in a daze, his whole frame trembling.

"Zinoviev, get up. We have orders to transfer you to another place."

Pale as death, he remained seated, saying nothing.

"Dress yourself."

He lay down. One of the jailers began to pull on his boots. Zinoviev did not move, but the sweat poured from his face. Another jailer passed his arm under his back and raised him. Zinoviev groaned and tore the hair from his temples. He seemed to have gone mad.

"Let's go!"

Zinoviev continued to groan, dangling his head. One of the jailers threw water in his face. Then he came out of his stupor and stood up.

"Take your things."

He began stupidly to collect his things. Half a minute later he was led out of the cell. A group of eight guards was waiting at the door. At this moment, Zinoviev understood everything, his legs trembled, he almost fell. They held him up, he resisted a little, with sobs and cries. At the end of the corridor he had a real attack of hysteria. Hanging on the arms of the guards, he cried like a woman. Lieutenant Evangulov ordered the guards to open a cell, which was instantly done. Zinoviev was pushed in.

The lieutenent took him by the hair with his left hand, made him bow his head and, with his right hand, fired a bullet into his brain.

This story has passed through the distorting pen of a journalist, but I recognize Zinoviev in it, and I can surmise the truth. A sufferer from heart disease, he dressed rather warmly, even in summer. When upset, he often tore his hair and went "mmmmmm . . ." with a certain grimace. In its high notes, his voice became effeminate. Seeing that he was being assassinated, the agitator made a supreme effort and cried out to his executioners: "Think of what you are doing. You are executing the revolution, the party of Lenin." On pain of death, the officer could not let Zinoviev speak another instant. He gave proof of initiative. He may thus have gained . . . the Order of Lenin.

This was the death of Vladimir Ilyich's oldest collaborator, his companion in illegality in 1917, the president of the Petrograd Soviet during the civil war and the Red terror, the first president of the Communist International. . . .

His brother, Radomysslsky, a young anarchist, had been killed in the Ukraine in 1920 by Voroshilov's soldiers.

The confessions — of terrorism, plotting, complicity with Trotsky, their former adversary — confuse only Occidentals ignorant of Russian affairs. They are cloaked in no mystery for anyone who has lived for any length of time in the atmosphere of the Bolshevik party. These confessions are in no respect different from the dictated capitulations to which in the course of the last ten years so many Oppositionists have been subjected, always in the name of the party. Such confessions are made out of utter devotion, and there is also an element of calculation about them. Smilga, an Oppositionist "capitulator," who has been in prison since 1933, once said: "We must retreat, surrender for the present, and when the masses awaken, we shall put ourselves at their head. . . ."

Zinoviev often said the same thing: we must remain within the party, even "flat on our belly in the mud," in order to be there on the day of the great awakening of the working masses, and not, by acting outside of the party, play into the hands of the counterrevolution. The only true thing in their confessions was their hatred of the leader, who must in the open be worshipped because to the world he was the incarnation of the party — the sacred party.

Their capital error was that their attachment to the past prevented them from seeing that this party is dead, and that — no longer with it but in spite of it and against it — the toiling masses will one day awaken and renew the fight for socialism.

I have read a curious document on this trial: the report of Mr. Rosenmark, published in the "Notebooks of the League for the Rights of Man" (*Cahiers de la Ligue des Droits de l'Homme*). The League's reporter holds in substance that the forms of Soviet law were observed and that there is no objection to categorical confessions. . . . We must hope, for the honor of an association that has rendered much service to humanity and has so high a mission to fulfill, that it will, in addition to this, not fail to publish the opinion of better informed persons. Mr. Rosenmark fails to examine the sole true hypothesis — that of confessions inspired by political devotion; disregards the fact that the material falsity of a part of these confessions has been demonstrated and is further demonstrable; disregards the principal explanation of the trial, which lies in the selection of the defendants; alludes to a Soviet legal code which does not exist, or if it does exist, has in this affair more than in any other been trampled underfoot.

Old socialist authorities, who are better informed, have formulated quite a different judgement. Friedrich Adler calls it a witch trial, and rightly reminds us that the witches who used to be burned at the stake commonly confessed their commerce with the devil. . . . He recalls that the falsity of the confessions forced on fourteen old Russian Socialists (Sukhanov, Groman, Ginzburg, Finn-Yenotaevsky, Sher, Ikov, etc.) in 1931 was irrefutably proved, and that Leon Blum had some strong words to say on the subject. . . .

Let us quote from Friedrich Adler:

In 1931 I had to make a thorough study of one of these trials, that of the "Menshevik Union Bureau," in all its details. From my knowledge of this trial comes my absolute certainty that the Moscow political public prosecutors systematically and deliberately extort fictitious confessions from the defendants. I will not express an opinion as to the other trials. Perhaps in these cases there were confessions that accorded with the facts. But as regards the Menshevik Trial there is no doubt whatever as to the fact of the false confessions.

At this trial, an alleged visit by our comrade Abramovich to Russia was the central feature of the "proofs."

The defendants made full "confessions" with regard to the details of their meetings and conversations with Abramovich in Russia in the summer of 1928, but for me it is absolutely certain that all these statements were made against their better knowledge.

We proved this in our pamphlet for every phase, and in the most dramatic manner of all by the photograph which shows Abramovich with the delegates of the International Socialist Congress in Brussels at the very time when, according to the "confessions" he is supposed to have been in Russia.

The overlooking of this congress was one of the "errors of stage-management" from which the Moscow trials continually suffer in spite of the most careful preparation. In our pamphlet on the Moscow Trial of 1931 we came to the conclusion that the "verdict" which provided the climax of the judicial farce was a pure invention as a whole and in all its details. We definitely declared:

". . . that not one single point of essential political importance in the tissue of lies in the Moscow trial can be maintained" (p. 35).

I have related above how the GPU attempted to incriminate me through false confessions. The examining magistrate who set this trap for me was the head of the GPU Opposition Squad, Rutkovsky, a citizen whose conscience, if he had the slightest vestige of one, would be singularly burdened. . . . I might, in this connection, adduce a few more facts of my own experience, but it will doubtless be better to recall an incident that is known to almost everyone who has lived in Moscow since 1928. In the course of the preparations for the trial of the provocateur Ramzin's "industrial party," the engineer Palchinsky — well known in Russian society, a former associate of Kerensky, one of the organizers of the Kropotkin museum in Moscow, a man of unbending character — was killed during the preliminary investigation. It was said that he had slapped an examining magistrate in the face.

One of the accused in a related affair (whom I do not name here because he may be still alive, though there has been talk of his suicide) was, after his conviction, visited by his wife. "Why did you tell so many lies about yourself?" she asked him.

"It was necessary," he answered.

The Social Democrat Braunstein, the old socialists Bazarov and Cherevanin, pioneers in the Russian labor movement, categorically refused to play the part dictated by the GPU and were imprisoned without trial. In approaching the more tractable defendants in the 1931 Menshevik trial, much use was made of the war danger. At a time when war was imminent, would they, as devoted socialists, refuse to sacrifice their conscience? Ikov, the only one of them who was really affiliated with the Menshevik Party, was broken by the arrest of his son who, the GPU led him to believe, was doomed. . . . In Verkhne-Uralsk prison, the historian, Sukhanov, one of the victims of this frame-up, who had delivered all the confessions demanded of him, revealed to his fellow-prisoners the inside of the whole farce, out of rage at being imprisoned despite the services rendered and the tacit or formal promises he had received. He went on a series of long hunger strikes and was ultimately taken away to an unknown destination (1934). It is not known whether he is still alive. [39]

Let us return to the recent trial. Nothing in it resists analysis. What are we to think of the confessions of Holtzmann who, with quiet dignity, refuses at the last moment to sign a petition for pardon, who employs his remaining words to express contempt for the agents provocateurs seated beside him; but who nevertheless confesses to having had meetings with Leon Sedov, Trotsky's son, in Copenhagen, where it is easy to prove that Sedov never set foot, and more precisely in the Hotel Bristol in Copenhagen, which had been torn down several years before? Was this not his way of crying out to the world— at the price of his life: "The whole fabric is false."

By so doing, he unmasked Yagoda, the high commissar of the GPU and the stage manager of the whole affair; and behind Yagoda, he unmasked the dictator of the low forehead.

As I have said, not one question of fact or of politics in this trial resists criticism; not one point would have resisted a two-sided debate. The whole business rests on the lies of defendants who have once again consented, out of attachment for the party, to sacrifice their consciences and their dignity; defendants who consider their lives guaranteed by precedent, Soviet law, and the service they are rendering to the leader, their enemy (their enemy in the party, not before the world).

The one episode in which we conceivably have to do with petty officials of the Gestapo conferring a favor on a GPU agent provocateur or a victim of agents provocateurs — Olberg — by enabling him to procure a Honduran passport, was, it can be proved, engineered from the beginning to end by Soviet authorities in Prague and elsewhere.

All in all, the method consists in selecting from among a large number of accused only those who are compliant, and placing them before judges who, in reality, are nothing more than executants appointed by the party to carry out the precise instructions of the party. The official documents show that the accused were in reality fifty-three in number: The cases of 1. Gaven, 2. Gertik, 3. Karev, 4. Konstant, 5. Martin, 6. Olberg, 7. Radin, 8. Safonova, 9. Favilovich, 10. Schmidt, 11. Esterman, 12. Kuzmichev are "reserved," says the official indictment. And to this day, five months after the execution of the sixteen, they are "reserved" in a total mystery. Why, if not because it is impossible to bring to open trial defendants who might become accusers and who must, therefore, be done away with in the dark? In addition, the indictment mentions the following, almost all of whom have been held in prison and in the most tragic obscurity:

1. The historian, Anyshev; 2. Arkus, a functionary in the Department of Finance; 3. Sharov, one of the founders of the party; 4. J. Shatskin, former leader of the Young Communist International; 5. Shliapnikov, Old Bolshevik; 6. Shtykhold, one

of the organizers of the Red Army; 7. the sister of Dreitser, who was shot; 8. Eismont, Old Bolshevik, former member of the government, imprisoned since 1932; 9. Fedorov or Fedotov; 10. Friedland, well-known historian; 11. Friedmann; 12. Furtyshev; 13. Gayevsky, a fighter in the civil war; 14. Gruenstein, sentenced to hard labor under the Czar, one of the organizers of the Red Army; 15. Hertzberg, an old party member; 16. Yakovlev; 17. Yatsek; 18. Lelin; 19. Udin; 20. Kuklin, one of the founders of the party and of the Soviet power in Petrograd; 21. Kunt; 22. Lifshitz; 23. Medvediev, Old Bolshevik of the workers' opposition; 24. Mukhin; 25. Okudjava, old Georgian revolutionary; 26. Uglanov, former secretary of the Central Committee; 27. Piatakov, former member of the Central Committee, member of the government; 28. Putna, military attache in London; 29. Karl Radek; 30. Riutin, former secretary of the Moscow Committee; 31. Serebriakov, former secretary of the CC; 32. Sliepkov, former editor of *Pravda*; 33. Smilga, one of the leaders of the uprising of October 1917; 34. Sokolnikov, one of the leaders of the revolution; 35. Jan Sten, former leader of the "Stalinist Left"; 36. Tomsky, founder and leader of the Central of Russian Trade Unions, who committed suicide during the trial; 37. the historian, Seidel; 38. and 39. Bukharin and Rykov, who were subsequently discharged for insufficient evidence; 40. and 41. Gogdan and Lominadze, both of whom have committed suicide.

Why have all these men not yet been brought to judgment? Will they ever be brought to trial (except to a star-chamber trial)? One thing is certain: that despite the half-darkness in which Russian trials are carried on, despite the mockery of the provisions for defense, and despite the totalitarian press, it would be impossible to try for these hideous frame-ups a revolutionist determined to speak, because any debate on the subject would leave the regime dishonored.

Yagoda, the chief of the GPU, was demoted for having framed the Zinoviev trial too clumsily. Thousands of arrests took place shortly before and during the trial, especially in government circles. Countless plots were discovered in the Ukraine, the Caucasus, Central Asia. Most of the known militants of the first years of the revolution were compromised and arrested. The entire generation of October was compromised.

A new trial was officially announced for November. It did not take place; the concoction was not yet complete. There was only the bloody comedy of Novosibirsk. Stickling, a German, and eight Russians confessed that, under the directives of the Gestapo and the Trotskyists (who were carefully kept in a mysterious background), they organized a catastrophe in the Kemerovo mine for the purpose of discrediting "our dear people's commissar, Ordjonikidze" and, in accordance with Trotsky's wishes, took measures toward establishing the advent of fascism in the USSR. This fantasy of a policeman's uncontrolled delirium served to justify the execution of six unfortunates, to prepare the ruin of several of the earliest revolutionists, and to provoke one more incident with Germany. *Poslednie Novosti*, the organ of the Russian emigres in Paris, which will not be suspected of sympathy for the Trotskyists, said the following on the subject:

> A witch may confess as much as is desired, that she flew through the air on a broomstick to a lovers' tryst with the devil and that she caused a hailstorm because he so commanded — we can only wonder how such confessions have been obtained (November 25, 1936).

Three men mentioned several times in the proceedings were the real target of the monstrous judicial farce of Novosibirsk: Piatakov, Drobnis, Muralov. They must be done away with. 40 Piatakov played a leading part in the sovietization of the Ukraine immediately after the revolution. After his capitulation to Stalin, he was placed at the head of the State Bank, and then as undersecretary of State, at the head of heavy industry. He was one of the most capable directors of Soviet heavy industry. Drobnis, a Ukrainian revolutionist, at various times a member of the government, likewise capitulated to Stalin. He seems to have confessed heaven knows what. Muralov, a great figure whom I have several times mentioned in these pages, had been in Siberia since 1928 and never capitulated. But in June 1928, from his distant exile, Tara, on the Irtysh, he wrote these words to Trotsky:

> I capitulate? I shall die, but I shall never capitulate. They can draw and quarter me, but I shall not capitulate. Even if I remain alone, I shall not capitulate. Formally, we are nonparty men; we shall loyally carry out any task with which we are entrusted, we shall use our meagre knowledge and our great revolutionary experience as best we can, and in passing we shall instruct the others, who are most frequently ignorant. But they shall not make liars out of us or drive us to passivity. They will do that no more than the Irtysh will flow uphill from the Arctic Ocean to its source.

There is also a possibility of a trial of thirty: about twenty
Germans — all *Gestapo agents*, who will of course have delivered the most complete confessions — and a few chosen communists, with whom a certain bargain will have been concluded — in the interests of the revolution, it is understood.
M. Pierre Berland, *Le Temps* correspondent in Moscow, thinks
is "most probable that this trial will not be public," and
"probable that the accused will not be shot."[41] They will disappear none the less. There is talk of trying Radek; Putna, hitherto considered one of the best strategists of the Red Army;
Primakov and Schmidt, military leaders and both heroes of
the civil war (Dmitri Schmidt is the legendary leader of a corps
of Red Cavalry formed by himself, a little Jewish worker,
to fight against the pogromists); Arkus, director of the State
Bank; Sokolnikov, Lenin's co-worker, former ambassador to
London, considered one of the first minds among the leadership; Galina Serebriakova, famed writer; Serebriakov;
Uglanov[42] of the Right Opposition, former people's commissar of labor. This would be a provisional selection from
among hundreds of political prisoners which the regime desires
to be rid of.

To do away with Zinoviev, Kamenev, the upright Ivan
Smirnov, was for Stalin to do away with the substitute team
that might one day take over the power as a result of circumstances impossible to forsee; the men he feared, though they
were all in prison. As for the others, permit me to quote here
what I wrote on this subject for a syndicalist publication:

> In connection with Radek, Piatakov, and several other
> leading figures of Lenin's time, we are faced with a problem
> of exceedingly simple political psychology. Despite every-
> thing, these men preserve a certain credit amid the flatness
> of the surrounding country; their names have become his-
> tory, and the masses could not hold it against them for
> not casting themselves heroically beneath the steamroller.
> Not only was the crime of August 25 (the execution of the
> sixteen), a dreadful, an unspeakable surprise for the mur-
> dered men; in addition, it sent cold shivers down the most
> supple spines. All those enabled by a cowardly smugness
> to retain their illusions with regard to the leader, suddenly
> saw the light. Whatever the Old Bolshevik generation may
> do or say, whatever lies the bureaucracy may persuade
> it to utter in the press or from the speaker's platform by
> invoking party fetishism, the welfare of the Republic, the
> cult of the leader — Stalin well knows that in its heart of

hearts this generation cannot judge him favorably. What
other purpose was served by the abominable articles signed
by Preobrazhensky, Piatakov, Rakovsky, Krupskaya (the
great revolutionists of yesterday, reduced to lickspittles)
except to establish between them and the leader a public
bond of complicity?

But here again Stalin finds himself in an impasse. This
forced complicity dishonors those who accept it, without
really making them Stalin's accomplices; everyone can see
that they are in reality his victims. And as victims, they
retain the right to judge him in their hearts; they acquire
the right to judge him someday before the people. The
great Bolshevik Party formed around Lenin was at bottom
a large family. Several of the most conspicuous members
of this family have just been done away with. Can the
assassin permit the others to live? "Dead men tell no tales,"
say the professionals in such cases. [43]

Rakovsky was not implicated. Like Radek, like Piatakov,
like all the former Oppositionists who have capitulated, he
too — the last to surrender in 1934 after six years deportation in Barnaul — signed the following paper as ordered on
the eve of the executions:

No pity for the Zinoviev-Trotskyist assassins of Kirov,
for the organizers of plots against our beloved leader,
Stalin, and the leaders of the party and the government;
no pity for the Trotskyist agents of the Gestapo. They
must be shot! [44]

His own situation is all the more precarious. If there is a
single word of truth in the confessions of those who were shot,
Rakovsky is just as guilty as they. If from 1932 to 1934 the
Trotskyists were engaged in terrorist activity, known and sanctioned by Ivan Smirnov, in prison at the time — and this is the
contention of the prosecution — what then is the responsibility
of the former ambassador to France who was, at that time,
the acknowledged leader of the Trotskyists? [45]

No one outside of Russia has been deceived as to the true
significance of this tragedy. Fascist papers in Italy saw in it
the triumph of practical realism over revolutionary utopianism
(*Il Messagero*).

In Paris, *l'Ere Nouvelle* wrote on August 26:

In reality the verdict handed down against Kamenev,

Zinoviev, and their accomplices proves that the Soviet Union intends to maintain the order without which it could not possibly pursue its task of organization. The Russian nation has accomplished important work in the economic field. Apparently it is not disposed to let this work be compromised by terrorism or even by the excessive desires of the extremists. Its prosperity, even more, its security, its very existence demand that things be so.

At the time of the Franco-Russian alliance and the peace policy of Nicholas II — the Hague conferences, if you recall — the press justified the hangings and deportations, which were, to be sure, far less numerous than at present, in exactly the same terms. The consequences are known. Is it then so hard to understand that such means cannot create a stable and defensible order, but that they most probably bear in them the seeds of frightful social convulsions to come?

No one, of course, exulted more than the counterrevolutionary Russian emigration. The *Golos Rossii* (monarchist) of September 1 said:

> This is the first time that we are pleased with an execution among the millions of executions carried out by the Bolsheviks. . . . They will not stop at Zinoviev and his associates any more than the French Revolution stopped at Danton. . . .

And on August 29, the *Vozrozhdenye,* likewise monarchist, dedicates these timely verses to Stalin:

We thank thee, Stalin!
Sixteen scoundrels,
Sixteen butchers of the fatherland,
Have been gathered to their forefathers!

. . . . .

Today the sky looks blue,
Thou hast repaid us for the sorrows of so many years!

. . . . .

But why only sixteen?
Give us forty,
Give us hundreds,
Thousands,
Make a bridge across the Moscow river,
A bridge without towers or beams,
A bridge of Soviet carrion.
– And add thy carcass to the rest!

TWO DOCUMENTS

Two documents were published by the Opposition in 1928, abroad and illegally in Moscow. In the ruling circles they had the effect of a bombshell, for they laid bare the divergences of views, the personal hatreds grafted on political disagreements, the unpopularity of the leader. Their perusal will help us to extricate ourselves from the gangster stories manufactured by the Stalinist police, to appreciate the true atmosphere of the inner-party struggles, and to estimate the underlying causes of what is happening. The prophecy in them has been fulfilled almost to the letter. All the persons quoted in these prophetic documents have been, or are in the process of being murdered.

Zinoviev and Kamenev had just been readmitted to the party after a period of suspension. Zinoviev was still in exile at Voronezh. Kamenev was in Moscow. Both of them represented the defeated Left, despite their break with the inflexible Oppositionists who had been deported or imprisoned. Bukharin, the theoretician of the party's right wing and the exponent of a moderate policy toward the well-to-do peasants, went to see Kamenev by agreement with his comrades, Rykov, who was still chairman of the Council of Commissars, and Tomsky, still chairman of the Central Council of Trade Unions. Of this conversation, Kamenev made a confidential resume, which he sent to Zinoviev and a few of his closest friends, and which ultimately leaked out. The text is rather long, and I shall quote only the essential passages. The document is in a sort of telegraphic style:

> *Bukharin:* . . . We hold that Stalin's line of conduct imperils the entire revolution. We may die with it. The differences of opinion between him and us are infinitely deeper than those which in the past separated us from you. . . . For several weeks I have ceased talking to Stalin. He is an intriguer without principles, who subordinates everything to the possession of power. He changes his theory for the purpose of eliminating this or that rival. In the septemvirate [there were seven members in the Politbureau] we exchanged the epithets of liar and bluffer. He retreated in order to be in a better position to strangle us. . . . I read a statement which I did not let out of my hands (he cannot be trusted with the most trifling document). His present task is to take from us Moscow and Leningrad and *Pravda,*

to replace Uglanov, who is entirely with us, by Kaganovich. As for his policy, it is as follows:

1. Capitalism has developed either by milking the colonies, by loans, or by exploitation of the workers. We have no colonies, we obtain no loans, our basis is therefore: a tribute levied on the peasantry.

2. The more socialism grows, the more the resistance to it will increase. This is idiotic and shows total ignorance.

3. If a tribute must be levied on the peasants, and if their resistance increases, we need a firm leadership. Self-criticism must not touch the top leadership, only the agents who carry out their orders.

In actual fact, self-criticism is directed against Tomsky and Uglanov. The result: a police dictatorship. It is no longer a mere question of finding a scapegoat; in reality the fate of the revolution is in the balance. Everything may perish with this sort of theory.

In reply to Kamenev's question: "What are your forces?" Bukharin gives names, mentions Yagoda. . . . This mention is certainly not unrelated to Yagoda's disgrace eight years later. "Voroshilov and Kalinin," said Bukharin, "betrayed us at the last moment. I think Stalin holds them by some special bonds we know nothing of."

> *Bukharin:* . . . If we do anything, they will strangle us by accusing us of provoking a split. If we do nothing, they will strangle us by means of petty maneuvers and will pin on us the responsibility for the lack of wheat in October.
>
> *Kamenev:* . . . And what do they count on to procure the wheat?
>
> *Bukharin:* . . . There precisely is the rub: they will simply repeat emergency measures as the difficulties grow (forced collections, that is). And that is simply war communism, throatcutting.
>
> *Kamenev:* . . . And you?
>
> *Bukharin:* . . . Perhaps we need a maneuver on a larger scale to conciliate the middle peasant. We may persecute the kulak as much as we like, but we must be reconciled with the middle peasant. But under Stalin and the idiotic Molotov, who keeps trying to outdo me in Marxism (we call him "lead in the ass"), it's impossible to do anything.
> . . . Let no one know of our interview. Don't call me

on the phone because they listen in. The GPU shadows me, and you too. I want to be informed, but not through secretaries and intermediaries. Only Rykov and Tomsky know that I have spoken to you.

Kamenev notes for Zinoviev:

I gave him your letter. He said after reading it: "I am afraid of documents." He is afraid that a document might sink him. . . . He is extremely shaky. Sometimes his lips quiver with emotion. For the moment he gives the impression of a man at bay (July 11, 6 o'clock).

Supplementary notes (night of July 11):

1. In general the impression of a man at bay. This is what he says about the whole mess: "Sometimes," he says, "I say to Yefim [his secretary]: Our situation is desperate. If the country perishes, we perish. If the country survives, and Stalin changes his line in time, we perish anyway. What can we do? What can we do in the face of an adversary of this sort, a debased Genghis Khan of the Central Committee?"

Bukharin says: . . .

4. If we begin the discussion, we shall be crushed for that. The Central Committee fears discussion. . . .

7. We cannot open the controversy, because then there would be a riot at once. . . . We shall say: There is the man who has led the country to famine and death! And he: There stand the defenders of the rich peasants and the NEP!

8. The party and the state have become confused. That is the misfortune.

9. All Stalin wants is to retain power. By giving in to us, he remained at the wheel. He will crush us later. What can we do?

10. Sokolnikov says: You must pursue a more active policy. Demand at least the removal of Molotov.

11. Stalin knows only one thought: vengeance. He stabs in the back. We must not forget his theory that vengeance is sweet.

12. Sergo [Ordjonikidze] is not loyal. He came and told us the worst things about Stalin, and betrayed us at the decisive moment.

And this conclusion:

Stalin's policy leads to civil war. He will have to drown
uprisings in blood.

The worst of all this is that Bukharin should have seen
things so clearly. The second document of the same type, dated
Moscow, March 20, 1929, reports so many facts unintelligible
to the average reader, that it cannot be quoted at length. I
shall quote only two passages. Piatakov advised against the
struggle against Stalin on the ground that it could lead to
no favorable results.

Piatakov says that he seriously believes it impossible
to take measures against Stalin: "Stalin is the only man who
can still be obeyed. Bukharin and Rykov are mistaken
when they think it is they who would take power after
him. It is the Kaganoviches who would rule; I do not wish
to obey any Kaganoviches, and I will not obey them."
Kamenev: What then do you advise?
Piatakov: Well, I have been entrusted with the State Bank.
I shall see to it that there is money in that bank.

At the end of December, Zinoviev and Kamenev defined
their attitude in these terms: "We must cling to the helm. This
can only be done by supporting Stalin. We must not hesitate
to pay him the price he demands. . . ." A few days later, learn-
ing of the banishment of Trotsky, Bakayev proposed that
they protest. Zinoviev went to see Krupskaya. Lenin's widow
answered: "And who would listen to us?"
These documents take us behind the scenes of the new Directory. Nothing makes more painful reading than these accounts
of the destruction of the revolutionary power. Personalities
occupy little space in them. Since politics is made by men, men
must be named; but it can be seen how far these men are removed from personal ambition. The Kaganoviches of whom
Piatakov speaks with repugnance and contempt, these are the
opportunists with neither scruples nor convictions, the late-
comers of the revolution. Piatakov was satisfied to be nothing
more than a conscientious bank director. He will not have to
take orders from the Kaganoviches who, knowing his opinion
of them, have now cast him in prison and are preparing to
kill him.
It is true that Alexis Ivanovich Rykov, Lenin's successor
as President of the Council of People's Commissars, and Bukharin, editor of *Izvestia,* were released for lack of evidence.
But on three occasions, at three different trials (one of which

in July 1935 remained absolutely secret), every effort was made to prepare Kamenev and Zinoviev for the executioner. Nothing prevents the case against Rykov (who has been demoted) and against Bukharin (who for the moment has been spared) from being reopened.[46] The very dismissal of their case was strikingly improper. It would appear that in accusing themselves and Trotsky, the sixteen who were shot spoke true enough for them to be executed; but that in making the same accusations in the same terms against Bukharin and Rykov they were lying. Tomsky, the third leader of the Right, did not await the developments: he committed suicide. Such was the contempt in which his persecutors hold the working class that they never took the trouble to tell us whether Tomsky died innocent or guilty. The discharge of his associates would seem to clear him categorically; and there is a Soviet law exacting the punishment as criminals of those provoking suicide by moral or physical persecution. What prevents them from applying it in this case? Tomsky, a Right communist, was one of the most moderate Bolsheviks. Fifty-six years old at his death, he had led a splendid life. He was a former lithograph worker, a member of the Reval (Tallinn) Soviet in 1905. After eight or nine years of imprisonment, several deportations and escapes, many years of illegality, he was, toward the end of the czarist regime, deported for life. Lenin's Central Committee entrusted him with the direction of the Central of Russian Trade Unions, and he had struggled to the best of his ability to give the unions, within the state, a real function in defending the workers' interests.

Rykov and Bukharin were temporarily spared only to avoid killing off all Lenin's Politbureau at one blow.

In totalitarian states the dramas of the tops are mechanically repeated all along the social scale to the very bottom. The Grober case, disclosed by the *Pravda* of September 7, 1936, as an abuse, demonstrates the pertinence of the 1928 documents to the 1936 executions. In 1927, Grober, a young communist in Rostov-on-Don, pronounces in his party unit a few words which are at once regarded as indicating opposition. Rebuked, he gives in immediately and votes as a good conformist. For nine years he works diligently, taking good care not to express the least criticism or the least opinion. The "campaign of vigilance" is launched. The order goes out to unmask any ex-Trotskyists who were insincere in their recantations, the Gestapo agents, etc., etc. An informer recalls Grober's pitiful little speech of nine years before, and our poor devil is at once expelled from the party. His brother, age nineteen,

and his sister, seventeen, young Communists and Stakhan-
ovists — hence model workers — in the Mikoyan factory, are
also expelled from the Young Communist League (and probably fired from the factory; Grober himself *must* be arrested).
The factory paper states that "we have spewed forth the last
vestiges of the counterrevolutionary Grober scum." Just imagine
the moral — and material — situation of the victims of this absurd
persecution; they can no longer show themselves anywhere. . . .
Three other young communists are expelled from the organization for not having "unmasked" the luckless Grober on time.
One of his brothers, a member of the district youth committee,
is expelled. . . . Two old party members, Polovitskaya and
Halperin, who years ago had recommended Grober, are expelled. . . . Two others, Vodolaisky and Denisova, suffer the
same fate for having been indulgent toward him in 1927. They
are all automatically expelled from the union too. Deprived of
work. Headed for the concentration camp. Fortunately for all
of them, *Pravda* happened to notice this time that the apparatus
was functioning in the void and that there was nothing, *absolutely nothing* at the bottom of the Grober case. . . .

But what if Grober had really said something in 1927?

THE APOTHEOSIS

The great throne room in the Kremlin, with its gilded columns, is crowded with delegates and guests. The obsequious
diplomatic corps is present, accompanied by military attaches
in gala uniform. Those of the fascist states like the rest. Delegates have come from the farthest corners of the Russian continent. There are Eskimos, Yakuts, Nentsis (who used to be
called Samoyeds) in white fur trimmed with red and black;
the peoples of Central Asia, Tadjiks, Turkomans, Uzbeks, Sarts,
Kazaks are there in long striped robes; Georgians, Adzhars,
and Agkhazians with engraved silver daggers at their belts;
Mongols, Buryats, Oysats representing a corner of China. The
scarlet silk bandanas of the working women are like poppies
scattered in the crowd. Decorated aviators, official dramatists,
distinguished mechanics, Alexei Stakhanov, Count Alexei Tolstoy — a crowd of more than two thousand delegates, all ears
straining toward the speakers' platform. On the platform are
marshals bedizened with golden stars and decorations, the
Order of Lenin, the Order of the Red Flag, the Order of the

Red Star of Central Asia; and the new parade uniforms, striped
with gold, of the Commissars of the all-powerful "Commissariat of Public Safety."

The next day every newspaper in the sixth part of the world
will rhapsodize as follows: "The twenty-fourth of November,
O day never to be forgotten! The most beautiful day of our
lives, the most beautiful day in the lives of a hundred peoples,
the most beautiful in history." (Approximately textual.) Stalin
appears.

There are no words to express the ovations, the hurrahs, the
thunder, the storms, the tempests, the hurricanes of applause.
The entire hall is on its feet, seized by a sacred frenzy. One
calm observer noted that this went on for thirteen minutes
and twenty-four seconds. There are Spanish anarchists in the
hall. They too applaud the dictator, the most powerful state
head in the world, who, along with everything else, has crushed
anarchism beneath the walls of his prisons. They know that
at this very hour Madrid is bleeding from all its veins. That
on the Aragon front their brothers are anxiously counting their
cartridges.

Workers' Catalonia, free Catalonia, this man can save you.
They regard him with eyes aflame, some perhaps drunk with
a sort of exaltation, some perhaps swallowing their rage. They
would gladly applaud not thirteen minutes but thirteen hours,
if only the militia could have ammunition.

He is a man of about fifty-five, heavily built, with much
grey in his hair. He is dressed in a military tunic, with neither
stripes nor decorations nor insignia, and military boots. No
one here is more simply dressed, and his simplicity contrasts
sharply with the regalia of the marshals and the high police
chiefs who, turning toward him with unctuous smiles, likewise
applaud him for thirteen minutes and twenty-four seconds.

He speaks for almost two hours on the new Constitution. He
speaks with few gestures. He turns to the Spanish delegation and
says: "Communism will triumph throughout the world!" Applause! That is a good sign. Madrid will be saved, Barcelona
will be saved. People of Spain, he said that. . . . But next day
this exclamation is suppressed in the reports. A bad sign.
Had he changed his mind? They are worried. Had they of-
fended him?

He announces that nothing will change. One party, one word,
one chief. Secret ballot as in Germany or Italy. He covers
with heavy ridicule the benighted foreign critics of the Constitution. In the Soviet Union no one criticized it. No one. He regards one amendment as justified, and it is added to the basic

law. The law guarantees personal property and inheritance. Every time he pauses, two thousand men stand and applaud. Applause after he has finished. The Nentsis, the Uzbeks, the Turkomans, the Eskimos, the Yakuts, the Tadzhiks, the *kolkhozniki* who have come to this stupendous festival from the tundras and the steppes exult: they have seen the incomparable leader.

Delegations bring their presents to him on the platform. The finest is that of the mechanical engineers, the precision mechanics shut up in some concentration camp: it is a giant clock which, in ringing the hours, shows three sculptured figures: Lenin, Stalin, and Yagoda, the former GPU chief. The symbolism is more profound than its builders imagined: the hour of Lenin, the hour of Stalin, the hour of Fouche.* But this marvel of captives' art and servility has in the political sense lost track of the time: Yagoda is in disgrace. Stalin smiles: in that smile lies the hope of pardon.

For days the monster cast files before this platform, all repeating his praise, receiving ovations whenever they pronounce His name. They all recite verses in His praise borrowed from the poets of their country; they all describe His power: everything that has been accomplished has been His work.

What has been accomplished?

Marshal Bluecher, commander of the special Far Eastern army announces the opening of a strategic road through Eastern Siberia, constructed by prison labor.

Admiral Orlov says:

> If we designate by 100 the strength of our naval forces on January 1, 1935, we can now state that up to the end of 1936 they were increased by 718 percent—seven hundred and eighteen percent—300 percent for submarines, 300 percent for small surface units, 75 percent for heavy coast artillery, 100 percent for antiaircraft defense, 510 percent for hydro-aeroplanes. In accordance with the requirments of the international situation, we shall build an impressive first-class navy.

Khrypin, the vice commissar of aviation, reports (November 29) that the Soviet air army disposes of 7,000 planes; 2,000 being first-class machines and 1,200 of these bombing planes. He says:

---

*Joseph Fouche was French minister of police during various stages of the French Revolution. He was noted for his unfeeling efficiency, his spy system, and his ability to save or benefit himself in any contingency.

Japan and Germany have set themselves a joint goal of 18,000 planes. We shall have 100,000 if necessary; our industry makes this possible. In a short time, we shall have several hundred planes with a speed of more than 600 kilometers an hour. . . . Even today, we could in five trips pour more explosives on the enemy than were thrown on Allied territory during the entire world war. . . .

Power. Idanov, representative of the Leningrad Politbureau, serves this categorical warning on the small states of the Baltic:

We wish to live in peace with all our neighbors, but if these countries place themselves at the disposal of aggressors against us, our Red Army will soon find means to broaden our window on Europe. . . .

Voroshilov announces complete victory in case of war. Ovations. Long live our first marshal, the victorious, the invincible! Tempests of enthusiasm. Liubchenko proclaims:

Let no one harbor any doubts. If the German fascists dare to assail the Soviet Union, the army of the proletarian revolution led by our first marshal, comrade Voroshilov [*Thunderous applause, prolonged ovation. The hall is on its feet.* Cries of "Hurrah, Voroshilov!" "Long live our People's Commissar, comrade Voroshilov!"], will inflict on them such a defeat as history has never seen.

"Only a sign from you, marshal," cry the Cossacks of the Don and the Kuban at the session of November 26, "and we shall fly to the frontier and wipe out the enemy to the last man. We shall finish him on his own territory! [*Prolonged applause. Hurrahs.*]"[47]

Krylenko, one of the public prosecutors, adds an important though superfluous note, saying: "There can be no question of freedom of the press, for the class struggle continues." What is this hostile class that still resists? Who are its members? What unutterable vermin is still attacking this power of ours, casting a shadow of fear over this apotheosis? The Trotskyists, the agents of international fascism, the hirelings of Hitler, Goering, Himmler—we have proved it, the military courts have made it clear, and the proof is sixteen corpses somewhere beneath the ground of this city, and five more in Novosibirsk. Tomorrow we shall prove it again and again by lining up more and more corpses! Khrushchev denounces

the enemy at home, "who frequently hides beneath the worker's blouse"; but will nonetheless be exterminated without pity.
Liubchenko continues:

> For the Trotskyists and the nationalists, the direct agents
> of fascism, the people has only one unanimous verdict;
> physical destruction!

A hundred speakers take up the chorus. In all there are three
ever-recurring refrains; We thank thee, oh leader! We are the
powerful, the most powerful nation on earth! Death, death
to these dogs, to the scum of humanity! Death, death! *Pravda*
for the thousandth time summons the citizens of the socialist
fatherland to vigilance in the name of humanity: "The socialist state of workers and peasants is the only humanitarian
regime. And it is precisely because we are moved by a humanitarian sentiment embracing all mankind that our state, supported by the entire people, will continue to track down in
every corner of the land, in their last hiding places, the ven-
omous monsters of Trotskyism-Zinovievism-Fascism, and destroy them without pity. We shall purify the life-giving air of
our socialist fatherland of their pestilential breath, and we
shall purify it to the end." [48]
So be it! Hosannah! Glory to the most humanitarian leader of all time. The novelist, Alexei Tolstoy writes that "humanity as a whole does not dare to dream of a constitution which
will offer it as much happiness as Stalin's genius has con-
ferred on the Russian people." A telegram is received from
Geneva that the *Freiheit*, the organ of the CP in Switzerland,
calls this Constitution "the greatest of all times and all peoples"
(November 26).
Svenska Dagbladet of Stockholm writes that "all the countries of the earth may envy the USSR." The *Times* calls the
Soviet Union "strong and prosperous." The *Daily Express*
publishes a picture of the leader and quotes his inspired words:
old England admires us. *L'Intransigeant* of Paris notes the
unanimous faith of the delegates at the congress in the leader of the New Russia. . . . "Long live the brilliant leader of
our great country, the creator of the Constitution, the great
Stalin!" Ovations. Hurrahs. And this happens every day.
Thirty, forty, fifty, a hundred times in every issue of every
paper. . . . Two million workers in White Russia sign a message in verse addressed to the beloved leader:

> *O wise master, genius of geniuses!*

Sun of the workers! Sun of the peasants, Sun of the world!
Power of rivers, glory and pride of labor!

Pravda goes on like this for five crowded columns.
Peter Vetchora, the Ukrainian poet, exclaims:

Stalin's greatness is a halo
Around the constellations of the firmament,
Around men and factories.[49]

The poet, Kabard:

Stalin, thou golden sun, thy name
Speaks the death of our enemies. . . .

The Georgian poet, Gaprindoshvili, sings His goodness:

He bends over the children
As a wise gardener over his flowers. . . .

The 1,487,000 inhabitants of the Karabakh territory address him again in verse:

O wisest and best-beloved father . . .

The Turkoman fishermen write to him:

As a lighthouse gives light to the fishermen
Of the sea, thy very name fills us with strength
And ardor. . . .

Etcetera. Etcetera. Let your imagination do its best in this genre. You will be far behind the truth. . . .
For His is the glory, the power, the mission.

FEAR

He returns home after these triumphs. He is guarded by the most reliable and most guarded men, who in turn guard and spy on each other. All his movements are secret. He is content. The machine functions admirably. The ovations, the motions of approval, the votes, the decrees, the laws, the resolutions, the central committees of the thirty parties affiliated

with the CI (we must not forget the Communist parties of
Colombia and the Philippines), the messages covered with
millions of signatures, the telegrams from abroad, the poems
of the poets, the love of the peoples. He has only to make a
sign to obtain the whole shooting match in the most flawless
form. The limits of praise are surpassed. The love of the
masses knows no bounds. The unanimity, the enthusiasm,
the faith, the exaltation surpass themselves. The Soviet Union —
or is it the Empire? — has one hundred and seventy million
inhabitants, all completely unanimous — like cockroaches. The
only trouble is that yesterday, or the day before, he ordered —
and paid for — the whole display, including the article in the
Zurich *Freiheit.* . . . So the ovations merely conceal a total
silence. Not a voice is raised without his command. Not a
gesture is made, not a telegram received. It is as if he were
all alone in the world, worshipping himself. He is worried.

Nothing anywhere is done without orders. Would nothing
be done if he omitted giving himself his orders? Can the machine not function by itself? Would nothing be done? And what
if this limitless obedience were only the false exterior of an
equal disobedience? All his orders, carried out to the letter,
become so absurd that the day comes when he must issue
counterorders. He says: "Complete collectivization"; in three
weeks his order is carried out, and the cattle are destroyed. He
is constrained to cry out: "Voluntary collectivization!" At once
the *kolkhozes* begin to empty. He must again cry out:
"Enough!" He says that science cannot ignore Marxism; and
treatises on obstetrics are studded with phrases borrowed from
Capital. He must intervene: "It is useless to intrude Marxism
into gynecology!" (textual). He orders new history textbooks.
And when he gets them, he has to publicly disown them. He
advises the party to search out the pasts of all communists
in order to uncover concealed Trotskyism. By the thousands,
the Grobers, their wives, brothers, cousins, their friends, their
neighbors are persecuted. . . . Enough! Enough! He desires
a proof of the affection of the masses. Two thousand signatures tell him that he is the Sun. Is it not barely possible that
they are making fun of him?

What do all these obsequious, supple-spined creatures in
their bureaus want? They want to live comfortably; what do
they care about socialism? But then what? Who can be counted on? If tomorrow the iron hand were no longer there to
hold the helm, who would take it? Nothing but weak-kneed
mediocrities round about. Voroshilov is still a sturdy fellow
of the Old Guard, even if he didn't invent gunpowder. Ordjon-

ikidze is more capable; he has read a good deal. But he is subject to attacks of conscience, though these are perhaps nothing more than nerves. The press receives a signal, and Ordjonikidze's fiftieth birthday is greeted with the epithets due an heir presumptive. There isn't much to choose between the two. And what of all these unknown lickspittles with the long, hungry teeth, insinuating, unscrupulous, without past or ideas, the men that he himself has called to power? Today he can count on them, since he has raised them up from nothing; and yet he is equally sure of being betrayed by them as soon as his hand weakens. . . . He is alone, alone. The last Bolshevik.

Is his life in danger? Whom can he trust? Are the men of his private escort sufficiently reliable? That they will never be. Several of them have already been shot, and the others know it. They are afraid. So far so good. But hatred is born of fear. They worship him. But what if a single one hated him? Distrust. Distrust. Has the Kremlin personnel been sufficiently investigated? A drunken worker said that. . . . Twenty-five floor-polishers in the government palaces are arrested (1935), all accused of terrorism. Syrtsov, a president of the Council of People's Commissars of the RSFSR* appointed by Stalin himself, conspired against him. Bazhanov, one of his private secretaries, escaped to a foreign country. His wife committed suicide. The best army officers are in their hearts Trotskyists — for it is impossible that they should not be. Radek, at Stalin's dinner table, said. . . . Piatakov said when drunk. . . . As soon as the tongues are loosened a little, hatred is revealed. He is afraid.

He receives the most secret reports in sealed envelopes which he himself opens. Here the truth is naked. Has nothing changed? For years the same old things have been going on. In the Verkhne-Uralsk isolator manifestos written by a Trotskyist group have been seized, in which it is said that Stalin by himself is nothing, that he can exist only through the support of the bureaucracy; that the upstarts of his regime form a new class of exploiters; that all the stages of treason have been passed. . . . In the Medvied concentration camp the Trotskyists are on a hunger strike. In the cell of one of them a letter addressed to Stalin has been found: "Traitor of the low forehead, I hurl my corpse in your face. . . ." In Suzdal prison, the old Andrei Borisovich, who can only walk

*Russian Socialist Federated Soviet Republic, the Russian part of the federation of republics composing the Soviet Union. — Translator.

with the help of a cane, was discreetly offered his liberty, a
sinecure, a tranquil end to his life, provided he recant. When
he was asked what he desired of the Leader, he replied with
an insulting snicker: "Let him resign, that is the only service
he can still render the revolution." In Moscow, a market woman
was arrested for saying that he was the people's misfortune.
Students in Leningrad called him the Gravedigger. The workers
in one factory nicknamed TOS (Tractors of Stalingrad) cig-
arettes, "Tomb of Stalin." "A tomb if you please," they said to
the salesmen, "sixty kopeks, and it's not worth more."*

Is that all? Trotskyists have distributed pamphlets in Mao
Tse-tung's army; Trotskyists have published a bulletin in Rio
de Janeiro. The Fourth International takes up the slogans
of the first three congresses of the CI. Trotsky writes. . . .

Traitor, gravedigger, fratricide, Thermidorian, destroyer of
the party: he is covered with disgrace. He is afraid. But one
thing in him is even stronger than fear: and that is rancor.

THE OLD MAN — THE FOURTH INTERNATIONAL

There is no other explanation for the mad proscriptions
which are destroying the structure of the regime, except hatred
and fear. Fear for himself, for the system, for socialism. The
system is not workable (and the secret ballot, a measure evinc-
ing mistrust of the petty bureaucrats, will not improve it much).
Socialism has been compromised. And he himself is at the
mercy of a centurion's madness.

The substitute team has been shot as a precaution. Only
the Old Man remains.

He is all the greater since not a drop of the blood that has
been shed lies at his door. And he alone remains.

Exiled to Alma Ata; banished to Prinkipo; interned in Norway; the butt of all conceivable insults and the systematic
revision of history; his name expunged from the dictionaries
and removed from the museums; all his political associates
in prison — perhaps massacred tomorrow in one way or another — the Old Man remains as he was in 1903 with Lenin,
in 1905 as president of the first soviet in the first revolution.
He remains as he was in 1917, with Lenin at the head of

---

*All these stories are authentic. — V. S.

the masses, in 1918 at the battle of Svyazshsk, in 1920 at the battle of Petrograd; during the entire civil war at the head of the Red Army, which he formed; at the head of a true party uncompromising despite persecution; at the head of an international party with neither masses nor money, but preserving the tradition, preserving and renewing the doctrine — a party overflowing with devotion. The Old Man is only fifty-seven — not so old at that. Everyone thinks of him, since it is forbidden to think of him; and he has everything that the Leader has not: a revolutionary soul, a brilliant pen, and men willing to go through fire with him.

As long as the Old Man lives, there will be no security for the triumphant bureaucracy. One mind of the October Revolution remains, and that is the mind of a true leader. At the first shock, the masses will turn towards him. In the third month of a war, when the difficulties begin, nothing will prevent the entire nation from turning to the "organizer of victory." Everyone knows how trials are made, and what the crown prosecutor's words are worth. A single gust of wind will dispel all these stagnant vapors.

All his life the Old Man has served the revolution with unflagging firmness and devotion. His very mistakes were made with so much honesty and passion that they do not diminish his stature. As early as 1920 he counseled the NEP, in 1922 he was for industrialization; and ever since 1923 for the renovation of the party through inner-party democracy and the struggle against the bureaucracy. In 1927 he foresaw the defeats of the Chinese revolution. In 1931 he stood for the united front of proletarian parties, which might have saved Germany from Nazism; he condemned the "economic adventure" of forced collectivization and the execution of the five-year plan in four years; in 1930 he foresaw that Stalin would decimate Lenin's party.

To permit his books in the Soviet Union would indeed suffice to make the position of the brilliant Leader untenable and reawaken the Bolshevism of the great years. Doubtless not a one enters. But where is the Chinese Wall that does not some day crumble in one spot or another?

The victorious reaction in the heart of the socialist revolution, based on a new privileged class, has brought about one more "turn" in the Third International: the conversion to bourgeois democracy. In the midst of a civil war in which the foundations of capitalist property are, by the very logic of events, continuously undermined, the Communist Party of Spain declares: "We are for the defense of Republican order and the

respect for private property." But President Azana, by no means
a communist, takes good care not to talk the same language;
he signs decrees confiscating the property of the rebels and
their accomplices. Changing its base, the Third International
passes from class struggle to collaboration with the middle
bourgeoisie; and at times this seems to be merely a maneuver
in a vaster complex of acts tending to the preparation for war.
. . . The Old Man, disposing of all the arsenal of revolutionary Marxism, opposes this Third International with the idea
of a Fourth. The new International is still weak, still in the
process of birth, and yet a ferment to be feared.

Let certain journalists call it a plot of the Gestapo, just as
their collegues used to call the Third International a Judeo-
Masonic plot cooked up by the Germans.

They will not prevent it, in case of war or a sharpening
of the class struggle, from becoming the germ or one of the
germs of a new Bolshevism, in the greatest sense of the word.

In Russia most of all. Stalin's fear and hatred, mingled
perhaps with a grain of remorse, are nothing more than prophetic.

And now everything is permissible against Trotsky. The
only thing that startles us is the successful blows delivered at
the right of asylum and at international law in general. In
menacing tones the USSR demands of Norway the internment
and expulsion of the exile — and obtains its demand. Never
did the government of the old Russian autocrats, harassed
by authentic terrorists, who lived unmolested in Geneva, London, Paris, dare to dream of anything like this. . . . Trotsky's
archives, deposited in the Institute for Social History in Paris,
were stolen last November by adroit specialists, equipped with
acetylene blowtorches, and having an automobile at their disposal. They carried out their orders to the letter, touching
nothing else. Have no fear; they will never be caught. When
Mexico consented to grant asylum to the man for whom "the
planet is without a visa," the Communist Party of that country
announced that it would provoke disturbances to prevent his
landing. . . . When, in Paris, the International Bureau for the
Right of Asylum is requested to express itself on the scandal
of Trotsky's internment in Norway, it politely replies that
it is interested solely in the victims of fascism. Does this Bureau not think that the socialists, the anarchists, and the communists banished from the USSR after having been persecuted there, are not entitled to the same rights as the refugees
from Germany and Italy? That is a strange point of view,
the logic of the Stalinist "liberal."

AMBUSH IN SPAIN

The world today is a composite whole. And those who fail to see that harm done to the revolution — to the workers — of the USSR causes suffering and danger to the workers elsewhere, must be exceedingly blind. Whether we like it or not, the social changes which today we are watching and participating in do not stop at borderlines, most of which are artificial or obsolete. Hardly had Stalin got rid of his possible rivals by executing the sixteen, thus, as he thought, assuring the rightward development of bureaucratic communism, than the class war broke out in Spain and placed him in the most delicate situation.

First he kept his hands off. No complications! The success of the Spanish fascists, the menace to Madrid, forced him to abandon his reserve. The victory of Franco in Spain would mean the encirclement of France, the ally of the USSR. The entire European balance of power would be shifted to the profit of Germany. That was his first reason for intervening.

And here is the second: To put to death the companions of Lenin, to decimate the old party, and to stand idly by while the working class of Spain was being massacred, would have been to cast aside the mask, to offer the most serious food for Trotskyist criticism, and to compromise even his remaining semblance of revolutionary prestige; while to appear before the Russian people and the working class of the world as the savior of Spanish democracy, would compensate for plenty of misdeeds and politically consolidate his regime.

After two months of strict nonintervention, Stalin makes up his mind. Rosenberg arrives in Madrid, Antonov-Ovseenko in Barcelona. Cargoes are landed at Cartagena and elsewhere. This is not a breach of the nonintervention pact, it must be noted. Never did the USSR renounce the right of trading with the legal government. And indeed, Russia is eminently right not to permit itself to be swindled by the fascist states.

But is it only a question of defeating the rebel generals, as some people pretend to believe? Are we not rather on the threshold of a proletarian revolution? Are we simply going to save the republic that supported these generals, maintained their army, and prepared this attempt at preventive counter-revolution? Or are we going to establish a different, totally different republic?

111

The question is not theoretical. Its solution depends on no individual, but is being solved by events. Already in Madrid, Valencia, Barcelona, it has been necessary to confiscate and collectivize the property of the fascist murderers. Actually, the entire production of Catalonia, the industrial heart of Iberia, is administered by the unions. The militia was formed by the workers' organizations. Anarchists participate in the power. Is the working class of Spain shedding its blood only in order to abdicate its power after winning the most costly victories?

The war is dragging out, the sufferings of the masses are increasing. Two sorts of measures will be necessary to the reconstruction: a directed economy and rationing. By whom is this economy to be directed, and for whose benefit? And what sort of rationing? Is a directed economy contemplated in which the workers, receiving the shortest rations, will work for the benefit of a minority of capitalists and landowners, who will have returned from Paris, Genoa, Rome, and Lisbon after the bombardments are over? That would not be so easy to put over. Or is the new economy to be for the benefit of the collectivity, directed by those who have made the greatest sacrifices and accomplished the greatest feats of bravery? The word is socialism. The dilemma is: fascism or socialism. As for the intermediary position, the reactionaries have forfeited it; the working class, the peasants, the middle class do not need it.

I do not believe I am speaking like a doctrinaire. I am seeking only to unravel the meaning of events determined by mass forces. By attempting to go against the current, it will be possible only to provoke unnecessary struggles and sufferings; or the victory of fascism in one form or another.

The role of a great socialist power under these circumstances could be decisive. But what is the role of the Stalinist power?

The newspapers and the party press maintain a strange silence on certain points. Likewise the intellectuals: and without doubt for the same reason. But these matters are not strategic secrets, and they are known to the enemy. It is chiefly from the working class that they must be concealed.

There is in Spain an important communist opposition party, that is, a party hostile to the Stalinist conception of socialism, to the totalitarian state, and the bureaucratic system: the *Partido Obrero de Unificacion Marxista,* the POUM for short. Its founders, Joaquin Maurin, Andres Nin, Gorkin, Andrade, have all been expelled from the Communist International. Maurin was shot by the rebels.[50] This party has lost many of its best men in the fighting: Etchebehere, the leader of its first motorized column, who fell on the Madrid front; Jose Oliver, killed in Galicia; Germinal Vidal and Pedro Villarosa, in Aragon. Next to the CNT, it has lost more men than any other party.

In October the POUM formed a youth group under the name of Communist Youth of Iberia. The Stalinist communists in Catalonia and in the Madrid youth movement call themselves — out of irony, no doubt, and for the purpose of confusion — socialists. In their press they denounce the foundation of the POUM youth organization as a treasonous, profascist maneuver. They talk of "making the traitors feel their iron hand" (sic). And more. With impunity, a gang of them loot the youth local in Madrid.

This is the first intrusion of Stalinist ethics into the revolutionary democracy of Spain.

When the Madrid defense junta was formed, the only committee which did not leave the capital was that of the POUM. Yet the POUM has been excluded from the defense junta, although it represents thousands of fighters in the front line. The socialist, syndicalist, and anarchist fighters inform the delegates from the Executive Committee of the POUM that it was the twofold pressure of the Stalinist party and of the Soviet legation which brought about its exclusion, in opposition to the opinion of the great majority of the Spanish fighters.

La Batalla of Barcelona, the central organ of the POUM, reported on November 27 with admirable moderation this unheard-of situation:

> It is intolerable that in lending us a certain aid, they presume to impose on us certain political forms, to pronounce vetoes and actually direct Spanish politics.

Meanwhile, the Madrid organ of the POUM had been suspended. We understand that Stalinist pressure achieved this first crime against freedom of opinion in the revolutionary democracy of Spain.

After *La Batalla* had revealed this brutal intrusion of Soviet diplomacy into the political life of the Spanish workers, the Soviet Consulate in Barcelona replied with a note to the press in which it denounced this paper as "sold to international fascism." This is the beginning of a campaign of calumny whose motives and journalistic delirium can be surmised. *Treball*, the organ of the PSUC, the Unified Socialist Party of Catalonia affiliated to the Third International, denounces the POUM militia as the "agents of Franco-Hitler-Mussolini," not without adding that they are Trotskyists, and consequently agents of the Gestapo, "as has been proved in the trials of Moscow and Novosibirsk. . . " (quoted literally). Everything is interrelated. These infamies lead from one end of Europe to the other. It turns out that the old Russian revolutionists were shot in order to facilitate the strangling of the Spanish revolutionists.

It is useless here to report the countless petty incidents (the use of the radio, the censorship, the press) showing the use of the bureaus of the Catalonian Generalidad by a party unscrupulously pursuing its policy of crushing another proletarian party. After a number of intrigues, the abscess bursts. The PSUC provokes the resignation of the Council of the Generalidad, demanding the exclusion of the POUM from the government and finally from the antifascist bloc (middle of December). Comorera of the PSUC denounces extremism in his interviews, and demands a strong government from which the "insulters of the USSR" will be excluded.

The POUM has forty thousand members, of whom six thousand are in the militia. It will not be easy to crush it, especially in the face of the revolutionary loyalty of the CNT and the FAI, which cannot fail to understand that their fate is likewise at stake. They have perhaps not forgotten that Hernandez, the communist deputy, declared in Madrid on August 8 that after the victory over Franco "we will settle our accounts with the anarchists."

No one will be astonished to learn that the Stalinist influence in Valencia is already stronger than that of the syndicalists, the anarchists, the left socialists, and the POUM. For this there are good reasons, motorized reasons, and the result is quite natural. But the uses made of this influence are astounding. *Solidaridad Obrera*, the organ of the CNT, revealed a truly serious state of affairs: "If our militiamen," says an article of the second week in February, in substance, "are unable to take the offensive in Aragon, the reason is that they lack the necessary equipment, while the conservative Catholic government in Bilbao is well equipped. This gives us food for thought. . . ."

I learned that on the same day mysterious influences had obtained the expulsion of the POUM from the Aragon defense junta though its columns have behind them the exploits of Monte Aragon and Estrecho Quinto!

At the bottom of all this lies a basic political conflict. Stalin does not want a fascist Spain, but no more does he want in Spain a workers' democracy which he is unable to control, and which would offer the world an example different from his. *La Batalla*, which is always extremely moderate in tone, wrote on December 15: ". . . The PSUC is not content with demanding our expulsion, but is for the pure and simple nullification of all the revolutionary conquests of the working class. To that we shall never consent. . . ." The Stalinists demand, in other words, a strong power against the working class.

From Lenin to Stalin the party has traveled a long road.

THE TRUTH IN THE SERVICE OF SOCIALISM

It is impossible to write all this with a light heart. But it is equally impossible to look on in silence. I like Charles Peguy for having written: "He who does not cry out the truth when he knows the truth becomes the accomplice of the liars and falsifiers." So many literary men have succeeded in keeping silence, gaily, with a supreme revolutionary elegance. They have found it possible to publish weeklies and monthlies and whole books without letting the truth glimmer through. That is a sign of great artistry. And it is a terrible danger.

Everything is at stake. Though the old world may not yet be crumbling — and on this discussion is possible — it is assuredly cracking in places. And at such a time, the clearest ideas that might guide us are falsified. The revolution seems to be turning against man, and particularly against the worker, assuming the implacable aspect of a totalitarian state, treacherous and bloodthirsty. Our greatest force, our greatest hope — international solidarity — is transformed into international intrigue, international persecution, vicious calumny in Moscow, Madrid, Mexico City. We have everything to defend, everything to save. And our foremost weapon is the truth. That weapon cannot be spared; the wound has bled too much. So much the worse for the lukewarm and the scoundrels.

The greater part of mankind, even among our adversaries, is today aware that the Russian Revolution was an event of incalculable importance, whose repercussions have barely begun to make themselves felt — an event which has changed something in the structure of the world. It is this confused sentiment which often makes them start back in anguish before the reaction they perceive in the heart of this same revolution. Yet the gigantic effort of the Russian masses from 1917 to the present time, the revolutionary will of Lenin's party, the extraordinary success of the Marxist thought that dominated and directed the course of history in the revolutionary days, have left behind them a society based upon the collective ownership of the means of production, a society in which man's very instincts are in process of transformation. An economy governed in accordance with a single plan has given proof of a resistance and a strength which seems without limit. The possibilities of socialism have been brilliantly confirmed.

After its victory in 1789-1793, the French bourgeoisie was to pass through several periods of reaction, several crises. Yet no one today questions the gains of 1789-1793. History has plenty of time. For history, the Russian Revolution has only begun. The day will come when the workers of the Soviet Union will look back on the Stalinist nightmare with the curiosity mingled with disgust which certain dismal pages of the past inspire in us.

Or does anyone imagine that the bureaucracy will indefinitely maintain its stranglehold on a young people of 170 million souls, which preserves in its memory the heroic legend of the great years — a people with a destiny to be achieved?

In the meanwhile we have neither the right to be silent nor to close our eyes. A sort of moral intervention becomes our duty. The Thermidorians of the Russian proletariat must be made to feel that we will not tell the pious lies that will permit them to elude their responsibilities before revolutionists and all men of good will. The time will soon come when they will deceive only those whom they pay. So much disapproval must be directed toward them that concern for their own safety will impose upon them a more human line of conduct at home, and greater honesty abroad. In the struggle between socialism and fascism, socialism will only conquer if it brings greater comfort and dignity to human life. It is this aspect which is most prejudiced by the bureaucratic reaction in the USSR. If we can force this bureaucratic reaction one step backward, if we can prevent it from committing one single crime by showing it as it is, we shall be restoring to socialism and revolution a little of their true grandeur and consequently of their ability to conquer.

December 1936.

Life and Culture

in 1918[51]

The shift among the advanced bourgeoisie was clearly reflected in literary circles. It may be said that every Russian writer had been openly hostile to Bolshevism.

We already know the attitude of Maxim Gorky, even he who had been associated with Lenin for years. We have seen him flay "the brutal socialist experiment of Lenin and Trotsky," which could end only in "anarchy and the free play of instinct." Gorky became one of the first to rally to the revolution, to recognize its grandeur and the necessity for its defense. He published the following general appeal:

> The experiment conducted by the Russian working class and the sympathetic intellectuals, a tragic experiment which may cost Russia every last drop of her blood, is a great experiment, a lesson for the whole world. In its time almost every people feels it has a messianic mission, feels itself called on to save the world, to give its best to the cause. . . . Come with us toward the new life we are building amid all our suffering and mistakes, without sparing ourselves or anyone else.

Leonid Andreyev, Ivan Bunin, D. Merezhkovsky, and A. Kuprin, the most influential Russian writers, who had all played the part of revolutionists under the old regime, remained unrelentingly hostile to the new government; but with astonishing intuition the poets grasped the deeper meaning of the revolution. In a few months time, the greatest Russian poets came over to the revolution and gave it a whole literature of exceptional strength.

The classicist Valery Brussov hailed the coming of the "just barbarians" who were to renovate civilization. Alexander Blok, the disciple of the mystic Soloviev, wrote the most popular and the purest of the masterpieces of the heroic period, *The Twelve*. Twelve Red Guards travel through the darkness and snow, arms in hand and preceded, unknown to them, by an invisible Christ with a crown of roses. . . . This Christian conception of the revolution was also to be found in the *Christ Is Risen* of the symbolist Andrei Biely, and in the profoundly orthodox mystic poems of Nicholas Kluyev and Sergei Yessenin.

By 1919, all the great prose writers were either very hostile or openly counterrevolutionary, with the exception of Gorky; almost all the great poets had rallied to the new regime.

With the exception of these great works, literary production was almost completely interrupted. If they wrote at all, the writers devoted themselves to politics.

In the working class and the party, the Proletcult movement (proletarian culture groups) was enlarged. The ambition of these circles was to renovate the whole of capitalist culture in conformity with the aspirations of the proletariat. They dealt with great problems. In the cities, they formed lively enough little groups occupied with the theater, poetry, and literary criticism. They produced only a few poets, and even these frequently fell into commonplaces about the factory and victorious work and proletarian heroism.

The class war raged also in intellectual circles. Men of letters refused to shake Alexander Blok's hand after he wrote *The Twelve*. Any association whatever with the Bolsheviks was infamy in the eyes of many literary men.

Almost the entire Academy of Sciences remained stubbornly hostile to the new government. It took years of hard struggle to break the resistance of the university faculties. The immense majority of the teachers were hostile; their trade union was only gradually purified and reorganized; the schools were conquered for the proletariat inch by inch.

The Commissariat of Public Education under Lunacharsky undertook a radical transformation of the curriculum. The old system of lower schools reserved for the people and high schools practically reserved for the bourgeoisie was replaced by a single work-school system. The old method of training subjects for the czar and believers for the Orthodox Church was succeeded by a necessarily improvised antireligious socialist program based on work instruction. It was necessary to prepare producers for intelligent social functioning.

They drew up a plan for combining school and factory. In order to better impress the equality of the sexes from infancy, the schools were often coeducational, boys and girls meeting in the same classes. But everything had to be improvised. The old textbooks were good only for fuel. The greater part of the old teaching staff resisted, sabotaged, misunderstood, and only awaited the end of Bolshevism.

The schools themselves were tragic ruins. They lacked paper, pencils, notebooks, and pens. In winter, the ragged children met around little stoves installed in the middle of the classrooms, where they often burned the remaining furniture to keep out the cold. There was one pencil for each four children; the teachers were starving.

Despite this immense poverty, a tremendous impulse was given to public education. Such a thirst for knowledge was revealed in the country that new schools, adult courses, universities, and workers' colleges sprang up everywhere.

Innumerable experiments discovered new and hitherto unexplored fields. Schools for backward children were founded; a whole system of kindergartens sprang up; and abbreviated adult courses put education within the reach of the workers for the first time. The conquest of the universities began somewhat later.

At the same time, the museums were enriched by the confiscation of private collections; extraordinary honesty and care were shown in the expropriation of artistic treasures. Not one single well-known work was lost. It happened that valuable collections had to be removed in the midst of riots, as in the case of the Hermitage collection; but they were returned safe and sound.

The scientific laboratories carried on heroically. Taking their share of the general privation, on strict rations, and without lights, fire or water during the winter, the scientists, whatever their political beliefs may have been, continued their customary labors.

In the evenings, the nationalized theaters played their usual repertories, but before a new public. The ballet corps gave performances during the terror which was exterminating the very aristocracy for whose pleasure it had been created; but the gold-decorated halls were filled with workingmen and women, with Young Communists whose hair was close-clipped to avoid the typhus-carrying lice, with Red soldiers on leave from the front. With the same voice that had once thundered

God Save the Czar, Chaliapin sang *The Song of the Flea*
for the trade unionists.

Expressionist painters decorated the public places for cele-
brations. Wooden or plaster monuments to the heroes of the
French Revolution and the founders of socialism were raised.
Most of these quite mediocre works have since disappeared.

The newspapers lost the richness and variety of democratic
times. They were gradually limited to three sorts of journal-
ism, all emanating from the same source: the Soviet newspapers, the two *Izvestias* in the two capitals, the Communist
Party papers, the two *Pravdas,* and the trade-union papers.

The winter of 1918-19 was terrible in the large cities, ravaged
by famine and typhus and lacking fuel, water, and light. The
water and sewer pipes froze in the buildings. Families gathered around little stoves called *Bourzhouiki,* an ironic deri-
vation from "bourgeois." Old books and furniture and the
woodwork and flooring from empty apartments were used
for fuel. Most of the wooden houses in Petrograd and Moscow
were torn down and used for firewood.

The interminable Russian nights were lighted only by candles and night-lamps. The toilets did not function, and heaps
of sewage gathered in the courtyards under the snow, ready
to cause new epidemics with the return of spring.

Long lines of customers were permanently stationed outside
the cooperatives. Vast illegal markets, periodically ransacked
by robbers, were held on the city squares. The survivors of
the former bourgeoisie came there to sell their last possessions.
Domiciliary visits and requisitions combatted the inevitable
speculation.

The blockade gradually killed off the weaker people. The
dictatorship of the proletariat did the impossible in looking
after the needs of the working class, the army, the fleet, and
the children. The former middle and wealthy classes were hardest hit by the famine. It was not rare to see old people fall
starving in the streets. The mortality rate, especially among
the babies and old people, rose steadily. The number of suicides, on the contrary, diminished considerably.

After chasing the dispossessed bourgeoisie out, the workers
took over their modern houses. Every apartment peopled with
armed proletarians, Bukharin wrote, must become a revolutionary fortress. Unfortunately, the comfortable arrangement
of the bourgeois apartments frequently made it impossible
to adapt them to the needs of their new occupants. Thus,
quarters were lacking for childrens' homes, for schools and

for community lodgings. The architects of the old regime had designed the houses for quite another purpose.

The Soviets instituted for the bourgeoisie the obligations to work in the form of compulsory public works. However, the bourgeoisie was largely successful in dodging this duty. In September, there were only four hundred bourgeois to be found in Petrograd for "rearguard work." Requisitions of warm clothing were undertaken. Every bourgeois had to furnish one complete winter outfit.

The legal recognition of free union, the facility of divorce, the authorization of abortion, the complete emancipation of women, and the end of male and church authority in the family did not produce any real weakening of the family ties. This destruction of obstacles made life simpler and healthier without provoking any noteworthy crises. Prostitution never disappeared entirely, but the disappearance of the wealthy classes who were its main support reduced it to relatively insignificant proportions.

Religious life continued a nearly normal course, although a certain number of actively counterrevolutionary priests were shot by the Cheka. The clergy was divided into two camps: the partisans of active resistance, led by Archbishop Tikhon, and the partisans of passive resistance. The Communist Party and the Council of People's Commissars several times affirmed that no obstacles would be placed in the way of believers.

The standard of living varied markedly from one region to another. All of the cities sank into complete darkness in the evening. Petrograd, the most exhausted and danger-ridden, lived an austere and calm life. The same privations were received more nervously in Moscow, already a bureaucratic capital, where the tonic air of the front was lacking. The cities of the Ukraine were prey to the partisan and robber bands, constantly pillaged and burned, devastated anew by every new occupant, and lived in a constant state of terror; a panicky clamor mounted over Kiev as evening fell. At times, it seemed that the bandits were the real rulers of Odessa.

An observer who crossed Russia in those days would have reported the singular and false impression of general hostility among the people for the Soviet government. This hostility was very real among the dispossessed, among the majority of the middle classes. Important as it was, the evolution we traced affected only the most advanced and intelligent elements.

The masses of the petty bourgeoisie in the country were too

close to the kulaks not to resent the attacks on the latter. In the cities, the petty bourgeoisie had formerly gained its living from its service and business with the big bourgeoisie, and its situation now seemed hopeless. Here and there, the petty bourgeoisie was more numerous than the proletariat, which was used up by the civil war. We are already acquainted with the modifications that took place in the social composition of the proletariat itself.

The proletariat was nevertheless the only element on whose fidelity the revolution could count. The individual worker was not able to see much beyond the small horizon of his own life. The education and information which might permit him to understand necessities, perspectives, and consequences were often lacking, and his selfish instincts resisted the higher interests of society when the latter demanded sacrifices. The workers suffered too much not to complain, to recriminate, to become desperate at times. The anti-Soviet parties made good use of this state of mind in their agitation. If the Russian working class was able to resist and finally vanquish all its enemies, the main responsibility rested with the Communist Party.

The party had only 250,000 members at the time, but those who joined were selected by history itself. It is true that a certain number of adventurers were to be found in its ranks, where they hoped to share the eventual fruits of power. Negligible from the point of view of numbers, this minority of false Communists did great harm, contributing to the discredit of local authorities. Thus, they appreciably facilitated Denikin's conquest of the Ukraine, where they gravitated to the granary. But the immense majority of the workers who joined the party volunteered for the civil war and accepted all kinds of dangers.

At times the working class became disgusted and lent an ear to Menshevik orators, as during the great Petrograd strikes in the spring of 1918. But when it was faced with a choice between a dictatorship of the white guards and a dictatorship of its own party, there was, and there could be, no other choice but that every last man took down his gun and lined up silently beneath the windows of the party headquarters.

The party saw, thought, and willed for the masses. Its intelligence and organization made up for their weaknesses. Without the party, the masses could have been no more than a swarm of men with imperious needs, confused aspirations, and gleams of intelligence lost in the mob for lack of a conductor to carry ideas into action on a vast scale.

By its incessant propaganda and agitation, always speaking the unvarnished truth, the party raised the workers above their narrow individual horizons and revealed to them the vast perspectives of history.

Every attack was concentrated on the party, and every defense force rallied to it. During and after the winter of 1918-19, the revolution became the work of the party. This is not to say that the masses were any less active in the revolution, but their activity was of a different sort. Thereafter they acted only through the party, in the same way that a very diversified organism makes contact with and acts on the outside world only through its nervous system.

A certain transformation came over the party as a result. It was closely adapted to its new functions and the new conditions. Discipline became stricter to facilitate action, purify the party, and paralyze alien influences. The party was really the "iron cohort" that it was later called.

Its thinking, nevertheless, remained living and free. The Anarchists and Left SRs [Left Social Revolutionaries] of yesterday joined its ranks. Since he had been wounded and since the German revolution had vindicated his policy, Lenin's prestige had grown even greater, but his simplicity still triumphed so that none feared to criticize or contradict him. His was purely the authority of universally recognized intellectual and moral superiority.

The former democratic regime of the party gave way to more authority and centralization. The needs of the struggle and the influx of new members who had neither Marxist education nor temper forced the Bolshevik "old guard" to ensure their own political hegemony.

A new code of laws was elaborated inside the party and, by extension, became the law of the newly formed society. It was a soldiers' and workers' law, founded on the revolutionary mission of the proletariat. Necessity, utility, conformity, and solidarity were its cardinal principles. It knew no better justification than success and victory. It demanded the constant subordination of individual to general interests.

Every communist and participant in the revolution felt himself the unimportant servitor of an immense cause. The greatest compliment one could pay such a man was to say: "He has no private life." Yesterday, at the command of the party, such a man was an army commissar leading the troops at the front; today he was a member of the Cheka ruthlessly carrying out his orders; tomorrow he might be speaking to the peasants in the country at the risk of being murdered in the night, or managing a factory, or carrying out some perilous secret mission among the enemy.

There was not a party member who did not fill two or three, or five or six, posts at once, and change around from day to day. The party did everything. No one discussed its orders. "Conformity to the goal" was the general rule.

The moral health of the party was reflected in its absolute honesty. It scorned the customary lying formalities and equivocations, the game of two faces, one for "the elite" and the other for "the masses." It scorned to differentiate between thought and word, between word and action. Everything was called by its right name. Ideas were clear and simple in their grandeur.

Idea, word, and action were all part of a single drive which was at once the cause and consequence of a clear proletarian policy. For social lies rise out of the desire to satisfy, or appear to satisfy, interests which are in reality incompatible.

Lenin and Imperialism[52]

At the time of the Second Congress of the Communist International in 1920, Lenin made the journey to Petrograd in order to speak at the opening session of the Congress. He spoke at some length, for two to three hours if I am not mistaken. Not in the manner of a public speaker, but like someone talking easily on a subject with which he is perfectly familiar, and who is anxious to hammer home an idea into the brains of his audience with blows of ever-increasing strength. He made no oratorical efforts. But he analyzed, described, appealed again and again to pure reason, and even more to sound ordinary common sense. He expressed no sentiments, but only adduced facts, impressive facts. He spoke with humor and frequently concluded his demonstrations by expressive gestures of both hands. "Do you understand?" He smiled often, and his face, conspicuous with its prominent cheekbones and powerful forehead, was constantly lit up by a sharp laughing glance, full of wisdom, which swept across the meeting, sought out faces, and received understanding from the faces when found.

I listened to Lenin, and as an old anarchist I had the impression that here the greatness of revolutionary socialism was revealed to me in a much more effective form than in the most convincingly written book.

In a few brief strokes, Lenin outlined truly colossal pictures. The word "millions" was on his lips oftener than any other. The abstract human being, the metaphysician, the individual of the anarchist scarcely existed for him. He calculated with millions and again with millions of human beings, with worldwide humanity, with the mighty *social* reality. He spoke constantly of the masses and brought the different races before our mental vision. Armed with Keynes's book, but seeing much further than this, he set forth the calamities which the Versailles peace treaty had already brought upon Europe, and those it is likely to bring in the future. Then he showed the surging up to new forms of social life of the races of Asia: 330 million Chinese, 320 million Hindus, 80 million Japanese, 45 million Malays . . . millions and again millions of human beings, impelled forward by the lash of the plantation owner, the whip of the slaveholder, and the machine gun of the agents of "civilization" . . . masses of human beings setting themselves slowly into motion. . . .

And suddenly we asked ourselves in amazement: "How is it possible that we socialists, anarchists, people of good will, could have failed to recognize all these great things for so many years?" . . .

Those comrades who read Lenin's short work *Imperialism, the Highest Stage of Capitalism*, now at last published in the French language, will receive, I believe, a similar impression to mine. This work, which was written in the year 1915, has lost nothing of its value since. The war, the "peace" of Versailles, the postwar period, the decay of reformist socialism, are only further confirmations of all Lenin's arguments of the year 1915. The scientific value of the methods employed by him is thus brilliantly demonstrated; for only one who is thoroughly conversant with and understands the play of natural and social laws can foresee events as Lenin has done.

Prewar times! The "socialists" pursued a miserable policy of vote catching. Party functionaries and deputies capable of seeing beyond the narrow limits of their constituencies or of parliamentary intrigue were few and far between. The anarchists declaimed the beautiful, unsophisticated truths which they had learned from Grave, Kropotkin, and Reclus, they fought against the old bourgeois society as isolated franc-tireurs, as dreamers, artists, vegetarians, or bandits. Syndicalism, joined by the most revolutionary elements of both tendencies, gradually developed simultaneously a theory and practice of class warfare. The world hastened along a clearly mapped out path toward war. The majority of those who held themselves to be revolutionists were in reality carelessly and blindly drifting toward it.

They were lacking in a scientific method of research and thought. But this method already existed: revolutionary Marxism. But with the exception of the Russians, a minority of

Germans, and a tiny minority of comrades to be met with here and there, scarcely anyone knew, or much less applied, this method. But that great things may be accomplished by its aid is clearly and indisputably shown by this little work of Lenin's on imperialism. The first thing which this work accomplishes is immensely to broaden and expand the horizon of all events. The petty happenings of daily life, the drama of your personal life, comrade, the ministerial crises — all these are doubtless of great significance, but they depend on infinitely greater things. The capitalist world is a whole, and in this whole the ministers and all individuals are like the infinitesimally small protozoa of the ocean. Everything becomes and passes away. We are no revolutionists if we cannot recognize at one glance the great main factors ruling all the others, if we are not thoroughly permeated with the feeling of mighty changes.

The capitalist state of society is a system whose mechanism and functions, which are controlled and actuated by fixed laws, must be known to us. The revolutionist requires nothing more than the simple statement of these laws, a resume of the facts, to be in possession of a superior armor, of an unshakable foundation for his convictions.

When, in the year 1915, so many of our comrades fought for "Right and Civilization" — and it is a heartrending fact that many deliberately took part in the war — when Sombat and Guesde were ministers in a cabinet of national defense; when Plekhanov advocated defense of country; when Kropotkin, Cornelissen, and Malato called upon the anarchists to lead the fight for "democracy" against "Prussian militarism," then Lenin quietly made his marginal notes to the works of the bourgeois political economists, took a row of figures here and there from their statistics and formulated his diagnosis. Here is a small extract therefrom:

"We are experiencing a period of colonial world policy which is closely bound up with the latest phase of capitalist development, the phase of finance capital."

This epoch is the epoch of imperialism, the last stage, the predatory stage, of capitalism. This is to be seen from the following:

Trusts are being formed, which replace free commercial competition by monopoly, by economic dictatorship. In the United States, the number of trusts in the year 1900 amounted to 185, and to 250 in 1907. In 1904, financial companies were in possession of 23.6 percent of all industrial enterprises, in 1909, 25.6 percent (more than one-quarter). In 1904, they

employed 70.6 percent of the total number of wage workers,
in 1909, 75.6 percent (more than three-quarters). The same
development may be observed outside of the United States.
International trusts are being formed. It is these which drive
the various states forward to the conquest of the world. In
1860, England possessed colonies covering an area of 2.5
million square miles. By the year 1880, the area of her colonies had increased to 7.7 million square miles, and by the
year 1889, to 9.3 millions. She now ruled over 309 million
subjects as compared with only 145 million thirty years earlier.
During this same period France's possessions increased from
0.2 to 3.7 million square miles, the number of her colonial
subjects from 3.4 to 5.6 millions. In the year 1880, Germany
possessed no colonies whatever. Nine years later, she was
exploiting almost 15 millions of black subjects. The distribution of the world draws to its close. But as the sharing out
is not such as to satisfy the greed of the various robber states
directed by high finance, war is bound to break out before
long over the question of a different division of the spoils.

Imperialism by its colonial policy thus prepares the crisis
which can bring about its own destruction — War. Imperialism
would certainly be destroyed by this crisis, and thrown by the
proletariat into the grave which it has dug for itself, were it
not that the effects of its actions spread like a cancerous ulcer,
and paralyze the revolutionary energies of the working class.
Lenin shows colonial exploitation to be at the root of opportunism and reformism, and quotes in this regard the letter sent
by Engels to Kautsky on December 12, 1882:

"You ask me what the English workers think of colonial
policy. Precisely the same as they think about politics in general. No real labor party exists here. Here there are only
radical conservatives and liberals, and the workers quietly
enjoy with these the colonial monopoly and the goods monopoly possessed by England. What is the result of this? 1. The
proletarian parties in England become bourgeois. 2. A section
of this proletariat is likely to permit itself to be led by elements
corrupted or at least paid by the bourgeoisie."

These facts in themselves may be evident, and yet a Lenin
was required to reveal this main cause of the impotence of the
labor movement to the masses, in the light of the revolutionary
fires of Russia. A Lenin was required to observe and describe
the importance of the colonial problem and of the new revolutionary movements in the East. Lenin is a revolutionary
genius armed with a scientific method.

The End of
Henry Yagoda[53]

The vast police coup d'etat begun by Stalin last July in order
to liquidate Bolshevism and to stabilize his personal regime
continues, and each day brings its new surprise. It will soon
be clear that the importance of this period of eighteen months
is not inferior to that of a Thermidor combined with an Eigh-
teenth Brumaire. The arrest of Yagoda is the sensation of the
last few days. It even casts into the shadow the arrest, which
has firmly been confirmed, of Christian Rakovsky, and the
rumors that Leon Sosnovsky, like General Putna, has been
shot in prison without trial. (Sosnovsky, the brilliant Bolshevik journalist, was so greatly appreciated by Lenin that
he made him his mouthpiece for the first pan-Russian Executive of the Soviets.) But nothing definite is known about this,
and perhaps nothing ever will be known.[54]

A government communique, signed by Kalinin, announced
the accusation of Henry Grigorievitch Yagoda: malfeasance
in office, crimes committed in the course of the fulfillment of his
functions. . . . What functions? Yagoda is an old Bolshevik
from before October, member of the Cheka; in 1928, he sympathized with the Right Opposition (Bukharin, Rykov), but
not for long.

. . . As head of the GPU for many years, he organized the
repression against the technicians, against every opposition,
in every sphere. Thousands of death warrants received his
signature. He ruled the vastest concentration camps in the
world — a position which gained him a decoration for the con-
struction of the White Sea Baltic Canal by convict labor.

He watched over Stalin, whom he was seen to follow step by step on ceremonial occasions. Chief Commissar of the Criminal Police, People's Commissar for the Interior, member of the Central Committee of the Party, commander of the special troops of the GPU, he was in truth the most dreaded man in the USSR, the one whose conscience carried — by order — the heaviest burdens: Chief of Police to the "genial Leader." In this case, he presided over the secret examinations (what horrible concoctions!) for the Zinoviev trial and over the execution of the sentences against the Sixteen. Immediately after the Zinoviev-Kamenev-Smirnov trial, his disgrace became known.

A scapegoat was required to shoulder the responsibility of this badly managed judicial comedy. Above all it was necessary to suppress Yagoda because he had become, in his turn, an intolerably disturbing witness. He is accused. Everything can be blamed on him: he committed — by order — all the crimes that are required, and he could commit no worse or unpardonable crime than to defend himself — for this could only be done by accusing others. He is irretrievably lost.

I picture him to myself in one of those cells in the Moscow prison of the GPU, which he himself had built, reading again the regulation which he signed, awaiting an examination, a judgment, an execution, the rites of which he knows by heart — understanding at last what he has done, what he has become, what those like him have made of the Revolution!

And I think also of Romain Rolland, who met him at Moscow and devoted to him such a handsome article. The great chief of the concentration camps and of those silent executioners in all the dungeons of the USSR conquered at a stroke the heart of the author of *Jean-Christophe.*

Is this not the occasion for Rolland to write a new article on Yagoda to try to save even this life — for is it not enough blood and too much cynicism on the part of the Master to attempt thus in broad daylight to suppress his servitors?

Already last September, I wrote: "The whole generation of October is condemned. Finished. Lost. Every one strangled in a trap. The few last survivors of the old Bolshevik cadres — the Litvinovs, Krestinskys, Bubnovs, Antonov-Ovseenkos — are also condemned, in the same way or by other means. Their existence has become incompatible with that of the regime."

Stalin's Terror Continues

with Envoy's Recall[55]

Antonov-Ovseenko, consul-general of the USSR in Barcelona, has just been named People's Commissar of Justice of the RSFSR. He is to leave Catalonia soon and return to Russia. It is well known that for some time numerous officials of the government of the USSR have been disappearing in entire groups. Here are the latest of the verified news reports in this respect, dealing only with events of the past two weeks: Goloded, President of the Council of White Russia and a colleague in the administration of the late Cherviakov, President of the Executive Committee, has, like the latter, committed suicide. The recent suicide of Liubchenko, President of the Council of the Ukraine, has already been announced in the press for some time. The government of the Buryat-Mongolian, the Tadzhikstan, the Uzbekistan and Georgian republics have likewise been purged by numerous arrests which were most probably followed by executions.

Furthermore, confirmed reports have been released to the effect that Jan Rudzutak, a member of the Politbureau and a Bolshevik of the Leninist generation, has been imprisoned. Sulimov, President of the Council of the Great Russian Republic (RSFSR) up to the beginning of the current year, is likewise in prison, assuming that he has not been executed in the meantime.

Of the three secretaries of the Politbureau of the Communist Party of the Ukraine — placed in office after last year's purge and following the fall from grace of Postyshev — two, namely, Khatayevitch and Popov, have disappeared.

A comrade who has just arrived from Russia tells me: "There were about a dozen of us celebrating the New Year in Moscow. All Stalinist functionaries, a few of whom can rightfully be called old revolutionists. . . . All devoted to the regime in spite of everything. Well, all of them have since disappeared, some are in prison, some certainly are not among the living anymore. . . . "

Well, Antonov-Ovseenko is going back. He knows just what to expect. We do, too. His disappearance is only a matter of time.[56] He has a fine revolutionary past. An officer, he took part in the Novo-Alexandria mutiny of 1905. Escaping from Russia, he emigrated to Paris, where he took up residence. A Bolshevik in 1917, he was a member of the Revolutionary Military Committee under Trotsky's direction, which carried through the insurrection in October. Antonov-Ovseenko led the assault on the Winter Palace and was the first to enter it. Shortly after that, he organized one of the first Red Armies of the Ukraine. Led the civil war struggle in that country together with Piatakov (shot), Kotziubinsky (disappeared, probably shot), Eugenie Bosh (suicide). From 1923 to 1927-28, he was among the leaders of the Left Opposition together with his friends Rakovsky (disappeared) and Piatakov (shot). Represented the Soviet Union in Prague and in Warsaw; in diplomacy, he was a collaborator of Rakovsky (disappeared), Krestinsky (disappeared), Sokolnikov (imprisoned), Karakhan (disappeared).

In Spain, he collaborated with Marcel Rosenberg, ambassador at Madrid, who has since also disappeared. He is an old revolutionist, once famous for his personal courage and for his rebel spirit; he was the last to escape, thanks to the revolution in Spain, among several groups of old Bolsheviks who were shot or imprisoned. He surrendered to Stalin in 1928 and has since made every effort to serve him well. But so has the majority of those shot or imprisoned.

On the day of the execution of the Sixteen, he wrote — on being ordered to, it goes without saying — an unspeakable diatribe against his former comrades of the Opposition, in which, outdoing Radek and Piatakov in his delirious prose, he declared that he had always been ready to shoot them. Taking his past into consideration, the Torquemadas of the Central Control Commission could hardly demand less of him. However, this type of prose has not saved a soul up to now. The fact that it is demanded of a person suffices to prove how suspect he is: marked for some future guillotine-cart.

Not a man belonging to this generation can be spared. All,

whether they like it or not, are considered in solidarity with the others; all are equally dangerous, in spite of their disgraceful self-vilification, to the new bureaucracy; for they are all equally conscious of the crimes of the genial Chief, whom they feign to adore while filled with boundless hatred for him. It is inevitable for him to order their suppression.

Antonov-Ovseenko will have to give an account of himself. He most certainly does not have any illusion about the dirty work he has been doing in Catalonia. Once the Russian Revolution was defeated by the bureaucracy internally, the revolutionists who rallied to Stalin out of weakness, short-sightedness or political cowardice have always sought refuge in Soviet patriotism in order to justify themselves.

They have said to themselves: Reaction has carried the day for some time to come but the Soviet country remains with its new acquisitions in history (collective ownership of the means of production); reaction will pass, the regime will change; let us work to furnish it with good equipment, good schools, a powerful army, etc. The bureaucracy can't prevent us from serving conscientiously.

(That's where they were deceived: it is much more concerned about its own interests than about those of the country; and the interests, being those of a usurping caste of rulers, have very rapidly become incompatible with the proper conduct of industry, with good administration in general, with the progress of education, even with the existence of a competent high command.)

In Spain, Antonov-Ovseenko only wanted to serve the USSR, but in reality he served only the bureaucracy. What does it matter, he probably thought, in comparison with the interests of the socialist USSR and its 170 million citizens, if the Spanish revolution is lost; it is far removed from the former geographically and in spirit; it is secondary from every point of view, Spain being only a small power. Stalin has a threefold aim there: to prevent a Franco victory, that is, the encirclement of his probable ally, France; to prevent a socialist revolution which could become a source of too many European complications and of social complications in Russia itself; to impose upon the Spanish Republic a sort of diplomatic and military domination. The patriotism of the ex-revolutionist Antonov-Ovseenko easily accommodated itself to this policy. But what sort of balance sheet will he be able to present to his bosses?

Among the assets: Stalinist domination of policy, censorship and military command; the weakening of the revolutionary proletariat (death of Durruti, assassination of Andres Nin, persecution of the POUM, imprisonment of several thousand members of the CNT); the defeat of the revolution begun in July 1936.

Among the liabilities: the republican victory compromised, the antifascist front broken; the government discredited; the Stalinists detested by all of advanced public opinion — from the radical bourgeoisie to the FAI and including the left socialists. A patent social crisis. For, certain methods cannot be used with impunity: the interests of a nation of workers fighting for their lives cannot be sacrificed to alien interests without punishment for the perpetrators. The new People's Commissar of Justice for the RSFSR, replacing the demoted Krylenko (who is also bound to disappear), knows this, sees it, feels that he is lost. He will nevertheless return: for it is necessary for him to go through with the bargain to the end, just as so many times in the past; because in ten years of capitulating against his conscience, he has burned all the bridges behind him, exhausted all his resources, lost all his chances of salvation; because he still clings to his hope of serving the Soviet fatherland, in spite of all the probability to the contrary. Finally, those who refuse to return have received an object lesson which is quite precise: it is the course of Ignace Reiss. A high Stalinist functionary only yesterday, he went over to the Opposition very courageously last June and was found on the bank of Lake Leman, murdered under the very windows of the Palace of the League of Nations.

The Condition of Women[57]

The equality of rights prevents neither physiological inequality nor the consequences, particularly irksome for the woman, of the general indigence. The compulsory promiscuity of the over-crowded lodgings is especially painful to the young girl and the young woman. How many couples are unable to separate because it is impossible to find different lodgings! In such cases the man liberates himself more easily, and forced cohabitation is less oppressive to him. The venereal dispensaries are crowded with infected youth who declare that they cannot be cured at home because of the impossibility of isolating themselves. The very low wage of the vast majority of young women forces them to seek a husband who is making good money, a military man or a party member. The surreptitious prostitution of all those who owe a tolerably good job to the amiability of store managers and office heads escapes, fortunately for the moralists, all statistical calculation.

Prostitution, properly speaking, subsists in most cities. Less widespread than in the big cities of the West, it is also more wretched. No legal regulation deals with it; in practice, commissions provided with discretionary powers keep it under surveillance and sometimes prosecute it; from time to time, on the eve of holidays or international congresses, sudden raids clean up Moscow, Leningrad, Kiev, Odessa. Hundreds of women are arrested in one night and sometimes they are deported by administrative measure to the North or to Siberia. There they fall into the clutches of administrators and the police.

The housing crisis and the repression of pandering make prostitution in the big Russian cities something at once infamous and sordid. The girls bring their clients to the rear of unlighted courts, to churches that are being demolished, to corridors, to abandoned gardens, to hovels. Night watchmen have been condemned for having rented to them the vestibules in front of the big stores. Bathhouses are sometimes their refuge. You can see the chauffeurs of trusts spending the night with their cars, picking up chance couples.

In 1928-1929 the Soviet press was ordered to suppress the section devoted to miscellaneous news. It has recently been re-established in the sense that the newspapers mention a burglary once a week in order to emphasize the promptness with which the guilty were captured. But in the days when the *Krasnaya Vechernaya Gazeta* (*Red Evening Gazette*) of Leningrad published, among other things, suicide lists, there were from twelve to fifteen a day; young women were the majority in these horrible statistics and they made free use of veronal which could still be obtained. We have no reason to say that suicides are less numerous today. The poverty which drives young women to kill themselves forces just as many onto the pavements. Extremely wretched, hounded by the militia and by the committees of the Housing Cooperatives, prostitution ends necessarily by joining the very numerous underworld, made up of burglars, swindlers, bandits, pimps, and guerrillas of all kinds. And the result is that if the same laws are not applied to it, at least the same rigors are. Deportees have told me of executions, by administrative decision, of "incorrigible" prostitutes, put on the same basis as habitual criminals, their companions of the depths.

There exist in Moscow (and perhaps elsewhere) one or more model establishments for rehabilitation. I once read a description of them by Mme. Margareta Nelken, deputy to the Spanish Cortes. This lady saw girls living freely in the nice House, studying there, and making as much as 300 rubles a month. In that period I met pallid women workers who worked like beavers for half that sum and dreamed of getting, by protection, a pair of rubber shoes from the store reserved for the GPU. . . . They did not understand that it was necessary to begin by prostituting themselves in order to gain access to a House where they might finally earn a living! Yet I admit that there is some laudable truth in the model establishments which tourists are taken to visit. But what a small place they occupy in life!

So long as the big majority of the young working women do not get enough from their work to feed, clothe, and house themselves — for it is not only a question of work, but of being able to live on the pay — the evil will remain without cure. If, in spite of everything, prostitution in the USSR has been much less important in the last few years than in most of the other civilized countries, it is due to the fact that it is more profitable and even easier to engage in petty speculation on the market or to steal from the shop than to patrol the streets. Moreover, the demand has diminished as result of the general indigence and probably, in the years of famine, of a physiological depression. As is obvious, these temporary causes are not the result of an improvement in the condition of women. Nothing is easier for a man supplied with means than to buy a woman, even outside the sphere of prostitution as such. *

The freedom of abortion, a capital conquest of the revolution, ceased to exist in the summer of 1935. Previously, circular letters had quietly strangled it. Henceforward, abortion is permitted only for medical reasons; and it is punished by obloquy and fines for the patient, by prison for the operator. At the same time the law grants premiums to large families. **
One sees very well, alas!, the reasons for this policy of natality, based upon the calculations of military experts who will tell you without blinking an eyelid how many millions of lives will have to be sacrificed in two years of war. . . . The return to obligatory maternity in a period of indigence is nothing less, for the woman, than an enormous aggravation of her condition. Then there is the matter of her rights and her dignity: socialism seems to us called upon to bring about the triumph of conscious and not of imposed maternity. Since the doctors received the order to advise against and to refuse abortions, the clandestine clientele of the abortionists has grown, the price of a medical abortion has doubled, with the result of an immediate aggravation of dangers, of suffering, of costs, and of servitude for the poorest among the women.

The new legislation has been justified by arguments which sound like bitter pleasantries. Do we not enjoy a free and happy life? No more unemployment, all careers open to women. Why should they spurn the joys of maternity? Things like this could be read throughout the Soviet press — which no

---

* This also exists in special forms, superintended and even organized, in the large hotels reserved for foreigners. — V. S.

** The encouragement given to large families is manifested in the allocations of 2,000 rubles a year for five years for every child beginning with the seventh and 5,000 rubles for one year and 3,000 annually for four years for every child beginning with the eleventh. These measures of serious support went immediately into effect. (Law of June 27, 1936.) — V. S.

longer publishes suicides. . . . Doctors have proved the in-
juriousness of abortions. On being interviewed, old serfs have
related their happiness in having had sixteen children, exceeded today by their happiness in living under the tutelage
of the well-beloved Leader. Nobody has raised the question
of the wage of the woman worker or of the condition of the
child.

Other legal measures taken at the same time put a tax on
divorce "in order to strengthen the family": 50 rubles for the
first time, 150 for the second, 300 rubles for any thereafter.
The absolute ease of obtaining a divorce often worked against
the woman, without a doubt; but do the officials imagine that
they have done well in keeping ill-matched couples together
by means of a fine? It may be expected that the legislator
will soon go back upon another great reform achieved in
the early years of the revolution: the legal recognition of the
free union as having the same standing as marriage.

The establishment of paternity, the compulsory pension pay-
able by the father for each child, with the amount fixed by
the courts, paid vacations during pregnancy and nursing periods (recently raised from 42 to 56 days before and after
birth), contraceptive freedom, the recognition of the free union,
the freedom of divorce, the freedom of abortion, the equality
of rights — these were what women gained from the proletarian
revolution. One can see on what points these gains have been
compromised, all the more so because the economic condition of woman and the place assigned to her in life by cus-
tom and physiology are still far from assuring her genuine
equality.

The social differentiation obliges us to distinguish the various conditions of Soviet women. The upper strata of society,
especially numerous in the centers, have produced the type
of elegant and indolent lady, who follows the fashions, the
theater, the concerts, who is desolated when she is unable to
get the latest dance records from abroad, who tans herself
every year on the beaches of the Crimea or the Caucasus.
I have heard the elegant in the literary salons praising the
enthusiasm of the Donets miners and the political wisdom
of the Leader. I have seen others, fat and dressed in trans-
parent silks, leaning on the arms of aviation officers, walking
past children with bellies swollen from famine who moaned
softly as they lay stretched out in the dust. Flies resting on
their eyelids and lips tormented them. The ladies turned their
heads away. After all, they were only little Kazaks or Kir-
ghiz. . . .

Below this feminine aristocracy is the average housewife of modest means, as needy as she is everywhere else. Still lower — and she constitutes a majority — is the woman of the people, a worker or peasant, who does the washing, goes for water to the fountain or to the river (in winter, it is to a hole punctured in the ice), takes care of the animals, raises the children, receives the drunken man at the end of the week, stands in line in front of the stores, buys a few metres of satinette in order to resell them and, thanks to this brilliant stroke of business, is able to provide shoes for the youngest. The foreign litterateurs do not come to question her while traveling. Disfigured and aged at thirty-five, she sometimes takes to drink. Then you hear her — on the revolutionary holidays — singing in a discordant voice the old popular plaints. After her fiftieth year she draws a checkered cotton handkerchief or a black one (according to the religious tradition) around her head and from time to time walks for kilometres in her old shoes over dusty roads, through mud or snow, in order to kneel in the only church that has not been shut down and which is always far away — terribly far away. . . .

The gains of the revolution would be immense in the realm of morals if poverty and the lack of freedom did not compromise them. For the woman, as for her husband, the whole problem comes down to two propositions: a rise in wages and a restitution of rights.

Managed Science,

Literature, and Pedagogy[58]

Social wars cannot be favorable to scientific research and to literary creation. They imply, in this sense as in many others, a sacrifice to the future. The material and moral enrichment of the masses is acquired only after the victory and the healing of the wounds. The intellectual production of Russia, therefore, was feeble during the years of combat. With the coming of peace, since 1922, life was resumed in the new order with an astonishing joy, ardor and variety.

Soviet literature was born in the two to three years from 1921 to 1923, with names known before and now renewed and enhanced (Serafimovich, Alexis Tolstoy, Mikhail Prishvin, Lidin, Ehrenburg, Marietta Shaginian, Zamiatin), and a throng of new names of young writers already full of experience and pith: Boris Pilnyak, Constantin Fedin, Leonid Leonov, Vsevolod Ivanov, Fedor Gladkov, Yury Tinianov, Mikhail Zostchenko, Mikhail Sholokhov, Nicolas Nikitin. A little later, or in the second rank, appeared Tarassov-Rodionov, Lydia Seifulina, Libedinsky, Pavlenko, Tikhonov. Within a few years poets produced magnificent work: Yessenin, Mayakovsky, Pasternak, Selvinsky, Tikhonov, Mandelstam. One is stupefied when one considers this glittering debut of Soviet literature, or records the audacity and the candor of the writer under a regime barely emerged from the terror.

Many of the works of that period would no longer be publishable today; they are, moreover, either withdrawn from the libraries or scarcely tolerated. Intellectual freedom is being extinguished in every domain with the victory of the bureaucracy. A period is opening up of increasing sterility, of spiritless official propaganda, of stereotypes approved by the bureaus as in other times and places by the Congregation: "literature in uniform," in the just words of Max Eastman.

It would be tedious to retrace the vicissitudes of this progressive suffocation. In 1929 two masterful writers of the young generation were suddenly denounced by the entire press, upon a slogan emanating from the Central Committee, as public enemies—one for having written about life in the provinces a novel of a realism designated as "pessimistic and counter-revolutionary" (Pilnyak, *Mahogany*); the other for having published abroad, in translation, a work condemned by the censorship because it was a strong satire directed at bureaucratic statism (Zamiatin, *We*). Pilnyak consented to all the desirable concessions and even rewrote his book in the optimistic genre. Zamiatin, firmer, was forced to expatriate himself. The young generation swallowed it all without flinching, even though Gorky, questioned by a Leningrad writer who wanted to know "if the moment has come to have ourselves deported," is supposed to have replied: "It seems to me, yes." Nobody had read the incriminated works, but everybody condemned them.

There is always an hour when the redeeming choice between cowardice and courage is possible. It was in 1929 that the Soviet writers abdicated their dignity. Their decay had already begun, it is true, and it required years, years marked by famous suicides: Sergei Yessenin, a lyrical poet, opened the funereal series; Andrei Sobol, prosaist and tormented revolutionist, followed him; Mayakovsky, social poet, renowned, rich, and loaded with honors, blew out his brains a few days after having adhered to the party's general line in literature. Young ones like Victor Dmitriev, passed away without noise. . . . Meanwhile, let us note, the writers have grown rich.

To work your hardest to create requires a tenacious courage that contrasts with the absence of any civic courage; and extraordinary faculties of adaption and mimicry. Some writers take refuge in the centuries gone by. There at least they are fairly tranquil. To this evasion of the present we owe some good historical novels (Chapigin, *Stenka Razin,* Tinianov, *The Death of Vazir-Mukhtar,* Alexis Tolstoy, *Peter I*).

In April 1932, the bureaucrats of the rod of the Associations of Proletarian Writers, who brutally lorded over letters, learned one morning from the papers that they were suppressed: decision of the Leader. All the old literary groups were to be dissolved and refounded—after a purging—into a new association of Soviet writers, directed by its communist fraction. The men of letters proved themselves docile. They had been enrolled, enthusiastically, into shock brigades, obliged to produce on an industrial scale works on the Plan. Regardless of circumstances, they had voted all the death penalties that had been demanded from them, they had sung the praises of the hangmen in verse and prose, they had paraphrased the most unbelievable indictments, they had demonstrated in the streets against the Pope and the Second International, they had promised in solemn resolutions to give the regime "Dneprostrois of literature"—to "catch up with and surpass" Tolstoy and Dostoyevsky.

. . . Without uttering a word of protest, they had allowed the arrest of all those among them who were scheduled for arrest. They had submitted to all the censures with a sort of euphoric resignation. And what censorship! Mutilated translations, bowdlerized biographies (the conversion of Rimbaud is suppressed from the Russian translation of J.-M. Carre's book, so that the Rimbaud case, in Russia, finds itself grossly simplified), entire works condemned. The Writers' Publishers of Leningrad was forced into bankruptcy under my very eyes, by the prohibition of several works, previously authorized by the censor, that were on the point of appearing: a novel on the NEP by Wolf Ehrlich, if my memory serves me well. . . . You would not believe it, the NEP having been obsolete (it was in 1930-1931). A novel by Roman Goul on the revolutionary terrorism of times past: it might have given troublesome ideas to youth. A novel by Helen Tagger: this excellent writer was not right on the line; in addition, she was the wife of a deportee. Poems by Kliuev: too much Old-Russian sentiment in it. The monograph of a danseuse. . . . Was that a time for dancing? The novel of Kuklin on the Red Army: deplorably realistic because there were drunken officers in it. . . .

The director of literary publications in Moscow told me in 1928, after having called upon me to abjure: "Even if you produce a masterpiece every year, not a line of yours will appear!" Thereupon the translation of my novel, *Les Hommes dans la Prison,* already set up in pages with the censor's authorization to print 10,000 copies, was destroyed. None of my books appears in the USSR. When I was finally able to leave Russia in April 1936, the censors withheld, along with my papers and personal souvenirs, all my handwritten works, the fruit of years of intense labor: an eyewitness account of the events that took place in France in 1910-1913, a novel, some poems. All of them were taken, in spite of the flagrant illegality of the procedure.*

Censorship in various degrees. The Writers' Union has its docket where every man of letters has a political label which is taken into consideration when deciding on publication, size of the edition, republication of his books. The editors pick a book to pieces before accepting it. The bureaus of the party, consulted in doubtful cases, sometimes designate functionaries to go over the work with the author. The manuscript then passes to the Board of Letters, attached to the Commissariat of Public Education, but in reality subordinated to the Secret Service. There it receives the necessary stamp of approval. Set up, the proof sheets are submitted to the censorship proper, likewise subordinated to the Secret Service, which casts a final glance at it, not without asking for all sorts of alterations if it so pleases. The work having appeared, it is not yet finished. It is up to the competent departments to recommend it to the libraries, which instantly assures it an unlimited sale, or to have it declared pernicious in the newspaper notes, which may mean its withdrawal from circulation. . . . The same works, the same authors, may be declared, in turn, excellent or detestable, for political reasons. Riazanov, the biographer of Marx, had just been consecrated as a great man in all the official publications (and his merits as a savant and a revolutionist are truly great), when he became irksome and was put behind bars. . . . The head of the cultural department of the Central Committee, Stetsky, immediately denounced him in *Pravda* as an overrated mediocrity. "We took him for a beacon," this blackguard writes textually, "he was only a candle." But with what can one compare people who are capable of mistaking a candle for a beacon? . . . Galina Serebriakova was still a reputable communist woman of letters on August 1, 1936, the author of highly esteemed works: *The Youth of Marx, The Woman of the French Revolution.* At the end of the same month, flung into prison on suspicion of concealed inclination to opposition, she is treated by the semi-official *Literary Gazette* of Moscow as a counterrevolutionist devoid of any talent.

On the other hand, almost worldwide reputations are built up in a few days by publicity methods borrowed from the

---

*The Italian communist emigration knows Gatto Mammone well, as an old militant who lived in the USSR for many years. For more than twenty years Mammone had been at work on a history of the labor movement of Europe. Taking refuge in Russia, he made the mistake of taking along his manuscripts and documents. **The Soviet censor robbed him of everything.** — V. S.

American trusts. The order need only be given to all the sections of the Communist International to have their publishing houses translate a seventh-rate work; the entire communist and communist-inspired press will proclaim its merits, and that may last for a certain time until it is perceived that it is nothing but a shabby fabrication. In the country itself, reputations are made as follows: Upon a sign from the bureaus, the communist cells in the factory start the discussion of a book, the "masses of readers" invite the author to lecture, the libraries boost him and so do the ships of the line; there is created a whole "spontaneous movement" which draws the admiration of old men of letters from abroad who are expressly invited. . . . Pilnyak never having succeeded in getting completely back into good graces, probably because he cannot help feeling and thinking like a man formed by the revolution, the favor of the Leader has granted first place in Soviet letters to Count Alexis Tolstoy, semi-official writer under the old regime, White emigre from 1918 to 1923, since rallied to the Soviet regime, rich and right-thinking. "My *Peter I,*" said Alexis Tolstoy to a Western journalist, "was printed in 1,500,000 copies and you won't find one in the bookshops. . . ." The author being paid at the rate of 350 to 750 rubles — according to his personal quota — per form of 16 pages and printing of 5,000 copies, it is not difficult to calculate that this novel alone, where it was believed that flattering allusions to the Leader could be seen, brought him millions of rubles. Besides — let us permit him to speak — "the state gives the writer all the material facilities. It procures him ease, rest, tranquillity, homes in town and country. . . ." The profession of encomiast of the regime is thus one of the most remunerative; here we are carried off in a sublime flight a thousand leagues from the poverty wages in textile.

Only, there are risks. At the exact moment that this interview appeared the Union of Soviet Writers purged itself, and sanctioned with copious applause the expulsion, arrest, deportation, and execution of a number of its members.*

---

*The terrible suspicion of Trotskyism thus befell Galina Serebriakova, Tarassov-Rodionov, Grudskaya, Trostchenko, Vegman, Selivanovsky, Ivan Katayev, Ivan Zarudny. Kamenev belonged to the Writers' Union, like another of those shot in the Zinoviev trial, Pikel. Long before that, those imprisoned or deported included: the poet Vladimir Piast (said to have committed suicide in his deportation); Ossip Mandelstam, one of the masters of Russian verse today; the poet Nicolas Kliuev; the poet Pavel Vassiliev (who was tried as a common criminal); the children's writer Biankis; the philosopher Ivanov-Razumnik, author of a **History of Contemporary Rus-**

In ten years literature and science managed by these police methods have shown their sterility. Not because there is
a lack of printing paper; but not a single powerfully inspired
work has appeared. Not a single Marxian work worth re-
calling in the country of triumphant Marxism. The last phi-
losophical school, that of Deborin, a dry and limited logician
who ruled over philosophy for years, was destroyed, some
time ago, by an administrative campaign. Deborin himself,
before becoming an academician in order the better to hold
his tongue, tried to commit suicide. Political economy? Rubin
and Finn-Yenotayevsky are in prison. Forbidden to raise the
questions of the exploitation of labor, of inflation, of the circulation of commodities, of the standard of living of the workers, of the per capita consumption of the population, of the
distribution of the national income, of what part of it the bureaucracy consumes, of socialism in a single country. History?
Political fortunes have been made by rewriting it to suit the
tastes of the day, like this Tal, author of the first history of
the Red Army in which the name of Trotsky is not mentioned;
like Lavrenti Beria who began his career by recasting the
history of the Bolshevik organizations of the Caucasus in
such a manner as to make a star out of Stalin. Anyshev—
author of a good *Essay in the History of the Civil War,* the
only one worth mentioning—and Nevsky—author of a history of the party, fairly good and withdrawn from circulation
for just that reason—are both in prison. In prison also are
the historians Seidel and Friedland, whose gentleness nevertheless remains inexhaustible. Maxim Gorky, after having al-
tered, in a sense unfavorable to Trotsky, the remarks of Lenin
which he had set down in his memoirs, was put at the head
of the editorial board of a *History of the Civil War* in ten
volumes, in which Trotsky is presented as the saboteur of
the revolution and Stalin as its savior. The *Memoirs* of Krupskaya have been done over again and edited by a special
commission which did not permit the widow of Lenin to write
a line freely. . . .

The Soviet encyclopedias are periodically revised in order
to bring them up to date in the political sense of the term.
In the second edition of the *Small Encyclopedia* you do not
find the forecasts formulated in the first on the consumption

sian **Thought** and of **Shtchedrin;** and many others. At the beginning of his deportation, Christian Rakovsky wrote a voluminous
History of the Revolution in the Ukraine, a work all the more important because its author took an active part in the events. This
work has not been published. — V. S.

of the masses at the end of the first Five Year Plan. . . . The biographies of the former leaders of the party vary from edition to edition. An encyclopedia of three large volumes, which cost the state years of the labor of hundreds of specialists and millions of rubles, was torn up entirely in Leningrad in 1932. The libraries are continually purged, and if the works of Riazanov and Trotsky are not burned it is only because it is found more practical to tear them up quietly.

The natural sciences? Geologists have been imprisoned for having interpreted subsoil qualities differently from what was wanted in high places: ignorance of the natural wealth of the country, hence sabotage, hence treason. . . . Others have been shot. Bacteriologists have been thrown into prison for obscure reasons. The most celebrated one died in a Leningrad prison hospital. But the further removed laboratory research is from social life and technique the more chances it has of being pursued without impediment and even with encouragement (grants, honors). All this still does not prevent the activity of the Secret Service. The subsidies generously allotted to the physiologist Pavlov for his researches into conditional reflexes did not prevent the arrest of his collaborators and friends. The encouragement given to the academician Yoffe for his researches into the structure of the atom did not prevent the deportation of his collaborators. The physicist Lazarev, after having been put in the very front rank of Soviet science, was imprisoned, deported, and then amnestied. *

Managed literature and science permit the organization of festivities at which solemnity is mingled with the mirth of banquets, with ordered ovations, and with ridiculous things that are at once amusing and saddening. The surgeons assembled in congress swear eternal devotion to the Leader. The gynecologists declare that they want to draw their inspiration from his teachings. The writers, whom he has called the "engineers of the soul," declaim litanies to him and adopt the canons of "socialist realism," which is actually neither realist nor socialist, since it rests on the suppression of all freedom of opinion and expression.

What is to be said of intellectual intercourse with foreign lands? The postal censorship pitilessly turns back all the publications, all the books that do not emanate either from official communism or a sufficiently tame and moderate bourgeois spirit. *Le Temps* is the only French journal admitted into the USSR, together with *l'Humanite.* Too advanced reviews, like *Europe,* arrived up to recently only on occasion.

* The historian Tarle suffered the same tribulations. — V. S.

In certain libraries the foreign reviews are put at the disposal of the public after all the undesirable pages have been torn out. Works of authors who are friendly to the USSR, like Andre Malraux and Jean-Richard Bloch, are prohibited. Moreover, a foreign author is judged exclusively by his attitude towards the Stalinist regime. Andre Gide, practically unknown to the Russian public and stupidly treated as a corrupted and corrupting bourgeois, becomes overnight a great revolutionary writer, only because he made certain declarations. For having scrupulously clarified his thoughts since then, he is insulted by the entire Soviet press. Foreign books enter with difficulty. Not a bookshop offers them for sale. The rare books trade is subject to censorship.

When I was about to leave, an old doctor to whom I was saying my farewell begged me to send him the journals of his speciality. "So many years gone by," he said, "and I haven't been able to keep abreast of anything." Suddenly he changed his mind: "No, don't send anything; they would think that I have connections abroad, and you know how dangerous that is. . . ."

At every turn in domestic politics, all programs and methods of education experience sudden transformations, not without resistance (usually simply inspired by good sense), which is broken down by administrative or police sanctions. Since 1935 there seems to be a desire to return to the old traditions. The students' committees have been suppressed, the directors restored, the discipline stiffened. The pupils will wear uniforms, as under the old regime. The organization of the Pioneers takes them in hand at an early stage in order to teach them the cult of the Leader, the goose step with drums beating, the holding of meetings of approval or of protest, according to the rules. A recent decision has instituted stable study manuals (up to now they changed virtually every two years), and Stalin has intervened personally to condemn the overly stupid popularizations of history and the overly maladroit falsifications. In this way, there are no history manuals as yet. So far as I can judge, however, the school programs appear to me to be much better than those of the primary schools of France and Belgium. Soviet primary school education corresponds more to a middle school education in the West oriented towards technical studies. The programs are more scientific. The conditions of the teachers, miserable until recently, were improved in 1936; a sustained effort is being made to clean and decorate the schools. It is not without results; but school materials are lacking, copybooks are rare, the pupils often work with one book for three or four; there is a still greater lack of educated instructors, and the perverse selection made in the pedagogical circles as a result of the repression only aggravates the evil. The school directors have to be appointed from among the party members. For want of communist pedagogues, the director is sometimes the most ignorant person in the school.

But the greatest evil is not the poverty of means and of men. It is the bureaucratic spirit that prevails in the schools and is translated into suspicion, informing, repetition of formulas devoid of all content, lessons of pure Stalinism crammed into children eight years old, stifling of any critical spirit, repression of all thought, and hypocritical dissimulation to which the child accustoms himself out of necessity.

NOTES

1. **Louis Auguste Blanqui** (1805-1881) was a French revolutionary who devoted considerable study to the problems of urban insurrection and military tactics. He participated in the revolution of 1830 and organized the unsuccessful insurrection of 1839. Freed by the revolution of 1848, he was again jailed after its defeat. Arrested on the eve of the Paris Commune, Blanqui remained a prisoner until he was pardoned in 1879, broken in health by thirty-five years in prison. Elected in 1879 to the Chamber of Deputies by the workers of Bordeaux, he was declared ineligible to take his seat by the government. He died on New Year's Day, 1881. His name has become associated with the theory of armed insurrection by small groups of selected and trained people as opposed to the Marxist concept of mass insurrection.

2. **Rosa Luxemburg** (1871-1919) was one of the outstanding leaders in the history of the Marxist movement. A founder of the Polish Social Democratic Party, in 1897 she began to participate in the German socialist movement and was in the revolutionary wing of the party, becoming one of the leading opponents of revisionism and opportunism before World War I. Jailed in 1915, she helped found the **Spartakusbund** (Spartacus League) which later became the German Communist Party. Freed by the revolution of November 1918, she helped lead the Spartacist uprising which was crushed in early 1919. She and Karl Liebknecht were arrested in Berlin in January 1919 by order of the Social Democratic government and assassinated.

3. **Karl Liebknecht** (1871-1919) was a leader of the left wing of the German Social Democratic Party. Sentenced to eighteen months in jail for high treason in 1907 for his book **Militarism and Anti-Militarism,** Liebknecht's name has become a symbol of revolutionary internationalism and irreconcilable opposition to imperialist war. He was the first member of the **Reichstag** to vote against war credits in 1914. Put into the army during World War I, he was imprisoned from 1916 to 1918 for antiwar activity. Freed by the November 1918 revolution, he was a founder of the **Spartakusbund** (Spartacus League) which later became the German Communist Party. After the crushing of the 1919 uprising in Berlin, Liebknecht was arrested and murdered, along with Rosa Luxemburg.

4. Leon Trotsky, **History of the Russian Revolution,** Vol. I (London, 1967), pp. 171-172.

5. Victor Serge, **Lenine** (Paris, 1917), p. 3ff.

6. **Gustave Herve** headed the extreme left wing of the French Socialist Party before World War I. He edited and published **Guerre Sociale** (Class War), signing his articles with the pen name **Sans Patrie** (Without a Fatherland). When World War I broke out, however, Herve renamed his periodical **Victoire** and converted his "revolutionary anarchism" into "republican" monarchism. After the war he was a rabid monarchist and reactionary.

7. The **Zimmerwald** Conference took place in the Swiss town of that name in September 1915. It was the first international gathering of antiwar socialists since the beginning of World War I and the collapse of the Second International. Participating in this historic conference were antiwar socialists from the belligerent countries as well as from countries that were neutral.

8. Serge, **op. cit.,** p. 3ff.

9. Lenin's speech on program at the Party Conference, April 24-29, 1917.

10. **Jules Guesde** (1845-1922) was one of the first Marxists in France and was a founder of the Socialist Party and the Second International. For many years Guesde was a leading opponent of revisionism in the Socialist movement. During World War I, however, he became a social patriot, supporting France in the war, and became a Minister without Portfolio in the Viviani Cabinet, August 1914 to October 1915.
Louis Malvy (1875-1949) was a member of the Radical Party who was Minister of the Interior in 1916. Soon after signing the expulsion order against Trotsky, he was himself expelled from France by the Clemenceau government for pacifist intrigues.

11. See Jacques Sadoul, **Notes sur la Revolution Bolchevique** (Edition de la Sirene), p. 76.

12. Quoted by Boris Souvarine, **Staline**, p. 184ff.

13. Serge, **Ville Conquise** (Editions Rieder, 1932).

14. Jacques Sadoul, op. cit., pp. 57-59.

15. British troops had landed in Archangel in 1918 and linked up with the White forces in the area. They were defeated by the Sixth Red Army in February 1920 and were forced to withdraw from Russia when Archangel fell to the Red Army on February 21, 1920.

16. French troops had landed in Odessa with the aim of occupying Southern Russia and aiding the White armies in the area. They were forced to withdraw in April 1919 due to the advances of locally recruited forces of the Red Army and the mutinies in the French fleet in the Black Sea.